THE UNIVERSITY OF WINCHESTER

Martial Rose Library
Tel: 01962 827306

1 9 NOV 2013

– 4 DEC 2013

0 1 APR 2015
0 5 DEC 2017
0 6 DEC 2017

SEVEN DAY LOAN ITEM

To be returned on or before the day marked above, subject to recall.

RECORDING
SKILLS *in Safeguarding Adults*

Best Practice and Evidential Requirements

Jacki Pritchard with Simon Leslie

Jessica Kingsley *Publishers*
London and Philadelphia

First published in 2011
by Jessica Kingsley Publishers
116 Pentonville Road
London N1 9JB, UK
and
400 Market Street, Suite 400
Philadelphia, PA 19106, USA
www.jkp.com

Library of Congress Cataloging in Publication Data
Pritchard, Jacki.
  Recording skills in safeguarding adults : best practice and evidential requirements / Jacki Pritchard with Simon Leslie.
     p. cm.
  Includes bibliographical references and index.
  ISBN 978-1-84905-112-5 (alk. paper)
  1. Abused men--Great Britain. 2. Abused women--Great Britain. 3. Records--Management. 4. Evidence, Expert. 5. Report writing. I. Leslie, Simon, 1952- II. Title.
  HV6250.3.G7P75 2011
  651.5'042--dc22
                                        2010018355

British Library Cataloguing in Publication Data ˙
A CIP catalogue record for this book is available from the British Library

ISBN 978 1 84905 112 5

Printed and bound in Great Britain by
MPG Books Group

Dedications

For the seven experts who helped us with this
book by giving their time, sharing their wealth of
experiences and voicing invaluable opinions.

Jacki Pritchard would like to part-dedicate this
book to the Angelou Team – namely Angela
Sands and Louise Perry – and to thank them
for their endless help and support.

Simon Leslie would like to part-dedicate this book to
all the committed safeguarding adults practitioners
in Berkshire who have worked so energetically
to put and keep safeguarding on the agenda.

Contents

Chapter 1

The Need for this Book and How to Use It

There are many different ways to safeguard adults who are victims of abuse, one of which is to use the criminal justice system. In order to do this, evidence has to be obtained to prove that an offence has taken place. Evidence can be presented in many different formats, one of which is written records. Anyone employed in the sectors across health and social care may not automatically think that one of their roles could be to produce evidence in an abuse case. The reality is that many workers may not even be aware of how prevalent adult abuse is in our society or that at some point they could be working with a victim or a perpetrator of abuse. Whatever job people are doing they should know how important written records are in their day-to-day work and that many of these records could be used in a court of law for different purposes (e.g. prosecution, litigation). Recording is important not only for the cases that go to criminal trial, but also for those taken through safeguarding, where proper evidence is still crucial. There is always the possibility that civil court action may be taken after following the safeguarding adults procedure. Therefore, the tasks involved in safeguarding adults work can be very varied because the term 'safeguarding adults' is generally used in a broad sense:

> This phrase means all work which enables an adult 'who is or may eligible for community care services' to retain independence, wellbeing and choice **and** to access their human right to live a life that is free from abuse and neglect. (ADSS 2005, p.5)

No matter what model of work is being adopted it is essential that comprehensive written records are kept and this leads to an explanation regarding why this book has been written.

Purpose of the book

The main aim in writing this book is to ensure that anyone who is working with adults knows how to record properly when suspecting or dealing with a case of adult abuse. For over 30 years it has been highlighted in child protection inquiries that communication has been a recurring failing (Laming 2003, 2009; Reder and Duncan 1999; Reder, Duncan and Gray 1993). Recording is a form of communication and it needs to be done to a high standard. Unfortunately many workers see writing records as a burden and do not understand why it is important to record accurately and regularly. It is of great concern that many workers do not have the opportunity to attend a training course which focuses solely on recording skills. Many line managers will say that they address recording in supervision sessions and that workers 'learn as they are doing the job'. That is just not good enough. Keeping records is an extremely important requirement in any organisation and a worker cannot record well unless they are told explicitly what is required of them. It is also important that managers read their workers' records. This is not about 'checking up' on workers; it is about making sure they are doing the job properly.

We acknowledge that some organisations do provide good recording training for their staff, but it is more common to find that workers' recording skills are inadequate and this is due to the lack of training and supervision. This book is concerned primarily with safeguarding adults so will address how to keep and produce records for evidential purposes. However, before this can be discussed in depth it will be necessary to cover some 'basics', which should fill in some gaps if workers have not previously had any in-depth training on general recording skills.

A lot of what is written in this book is plain common sense. It is here because sometimes workers make things complicated when they need not be. It is our hope that by stating the obvious a worker might feel more confident because they realise that they do have the knowledge already and are actually implementing it without realising it; others may realise they are recording correctly but perhaps could improve by utilising some of the tips given. Some experienced workers and managers who are practising regularly in safeguarding adults work might read parts of this book and question why certain things have been pointed out because they automatically do this in their own work. Assumptions should not be made that everyone practises in the same way. We want to remind the reader that practices in safeguarding adults work around the UK do differ tremendously. Although we have had national guidance from the

Department of Health in the form of *No Secrets* (DH 2000) and the Welsh Assembly's *In Safe Hands* (National Assembly for Wales 2000), practices in the UK are not consistent. Scotland has a completely different legal system and has introduced specific legislation to support and protect adults (see Mackay 2008). Therefore, one of our intentions is not only to spell out the obvious, but also to encourage consistency in recording which will in turn promote best practice in safeguarding adults.

We constantly hear that not many cases of adult abuse get to court, so consequently some managers and workers think it is pointless worrying about what might happen if they have to give evidence in a court case. One of the many reasons cases do not get to court is that records are so poor; they often fail the evidential stage of the Full Code Test (see Chapter 6) which has to be undertaken by the Crown Prosecution Service (CPS 2004). So the aim in writing this book is to make workers aware of how written records can make good evidence, how documents should be written and what needs to be kept.

We know that most workers are under extreme pressure with ever increasing workloads and there can be a reluctance to give recording the priority it deserves. Increasing workloads can be partly due to a lack of resources. It is important that people in positions of power argue for an increase in resources, but to do that arguments have to be put forward that there is a real need. Keeping good records can aid this. For example, a Safeguarding Adults Co-ordinator needs to report regularly to the local Safeguarding Adults Board which in turn is responsible for producing an annual report. The Safeguarding Adults Co-ordinator needs to be able present statistics about the number of alerts, strategy meetings, investigations, case conferences and an analysis of outcomes. In order to do this effectively, there needs to be accurate recording, for example completing all the forms as required in the local Safeguarding Adults Policy and Procedure.

The reader might find it helpful to read the findings of the Adult Protection Analysis Project undertaken by Action on Elder Abuse which commenced in 2004 and aimed to:

> investigate and develop ways of reporting upon, and subsequently analysing data, obtained by Local Authorities and other key parties, under Adult Protection policies developed through the *No Secrets* guidance. The intention was to establish a national recording system for incidents of adult abuse, with four key objectives:

1. To ascertain the current situation with regard to recording systems utilised by Local Authorities, Health authorities, Police and other relevant organisations co-operating under Protection of Vulnerable Adults Policies.

2. To develop recording and reporting systems that would assist in quantifying and understanding levels of reporting and incidences of Adult Abuse, thus informing Social Policy initiatives.

3. To test those systems in a number of environments to ensure they met national requirements.

4. To provide preliminary data during the course of the project on incidences and content of Adult abuse reporting, to facilitate Government planning in this regard. (Action on Elder Abuse 2006, p.6)

The following conclusions were made:

- Many local authorities were collecting large amounts of information on Protection of Vulnerable Adults referrals.

- Meaningful conclusions about data collected could not be drawn due to: no set time period; the lack of a standard format; differing policy, practice and intervention thresholds.

- At the time of request, fewer than 20% of local authorities who submitted data, had collected meaningful information on the outcomes of Protection of Vulnerable Adult investigations. (Action on Elder Abuse 2006, p.11)

Who the book is for

We want to state at the outset that this is not a 'professionals' book'. It has been written for any worker who works with adults across the sectors and at any level. Therefore, the word 'worker' will be used throughout the book as a generic term to include professionals, unqualified workers, volunteers, advocates. As stated above we shall go 'back to basics' in some chapters and some more experienced workers may feel this is not necessary for them, but we believe it is always useful to revisit and refresh issues at any time. These chapters have been included because we want this book to be helpful to workers who might be new to their job and know little about recording and for those workers who have had limited training. Other chapters focus directly on recording in safeguarding adults work and consider recurring difficult issues which present dilemmas for workers such as access to records, sharing information, consent and capacity, etc. Administrative workers will also find something for themselves in this book because we cover the importance of minute-taking. Minutes of safeguarding adults meetings (e.g. strategy meetings, case conferences) can be used as evidence in court and should be of a high standard. For many years minute-takers in the child protection field have been trained to a high standard; to date we do not see such standards on a regular basis when dealing with the abuse of adults. In some areas of the UK administrative workers are trained to do this job well; sadly in other areas resources are lacking and some chairpersons are still having to chair a meeting and take their own minutes.

Subjects covered

Many workers do see recording as an onerous and maybe unnecessary task. One of the reasons for this is that often it has never been explained to them *why* they have to record. Chapter 2 does this in the hope that workers will be encouraged to spend more time recording because there is a real purpose underpinning the task which might ordinarily be seen as very burdensome. Within that chapter the reader will be directed to where issues are explored in more depth elsewhere in the book.

Technology is developing rapidly; in the statutory sector computers and software packages are regularly used and updated. However, workers often struggle with the packages they have to use and complain they cannot write the records as they would wish to do. There is also much discussion nationwide about organisations becoming paperless, but the fact remains that the courts still expect 'original' or 'wet' documents; so many debates go on regarding what should be kept, scanned, etc. It is not the purpose of this book to consider these debates in depth but we shall highlight some of the issues and present some opinions and advice from expert professionals working on the frontline in the safeguarding adults arena.

Although workers within statutory organisations generally have access to computers, there are still many organisations which are not so fortunate and tend to keep paper (hard copy) rather than electronic records. Chapter 4 takes the reader back to basics and has been written for workers who keep paper records, but anyone using a computer should also read this chapter because it gives information about what constitutes good recording practices which should be incorporated into any electronic files which are being produced.

From Chapter 6 onwards the focus is on evidential requirements and how to meet these from the alert stage through to case conference. The reader will be encouraged to adopt a variety of tools and effective ways of recording (Chapter 5) and Chapter 10 will give essential advice regarding how to write a report for court.

Format of the book

From what has been said already it should be clear to the reader that this is a book that you can dip in and out of as necessary; it does not have to be read cover to cover. Because we have written this for a wide audience we are aware that the needs of readers will differ. We did not want this book to be produced in a training manual format, but recognise that the inclusion of some training exercises might be helpful. The format of the chapters is such that the crucial information and discussion are given within the body of the text, together with key questions, examples and best practice points. In several chapters exercises have been included which can be used on training courses or within supervision sessions and when appropriate suggested reading lists have been included at the end of a chapter.

Experts' experiences and comments

We thought it would be helpful to include in this book advice from experts who are actively working in the field of safeguarding adults. We approached people who we think are grounded and have a great deal of valuable experience. The people who agreed to help us have either taken part in an interview or written down their thoughts for us; they have also commented on the manuscript of the book. Their anecdotes and comments are included throughout the chapters at appropriate points. Two police officers have to remain anonymous, otherwise their views could not have been included. Our experts' backgrounds are described below.

OUR EXPERTS

Anonymous expert: A police officer for over 27 years having spent the last 12 years or so working in the field of child and adult safeguarding as an investigator, trainer and latterly as a co-ordinator within a referral unit.

Anonymous expert: Worked 15 years as a police officer. Has a full range of experience as a Detective Constable in various departments. Currently working in a Public Protection Unit primarily on vulnerable adult investigations.

Niall Baker is the National Head of the Business and Private Client Division of Irwin Mitchell Solicitors, a leading national law firm. He is a member of the firm's Management Board which is responsible for the overall strategic direction of the firm and delivery of its objectives. Niall has been with the firm since 1989 when he started work as an articled clerk, qualifying in October 1991. Niall is a private client lawyer specialising in Court of Protection work and the management of personal injury damages. He heads the largest Court of Protection department in the country and acts on behalf of many clients who are incapable of managing their own financial affairs. He has been significantly involved in the drafting of new legislation with regard to mental health and sits on various groups, giving evidence to both the House of Commons and House of Lords scrutiny committees.

Dr David Hewitt is a solicitor and a partner in Weightmans LLP. He holds Visiting Fellowships at Northumbria University and Lincoln University, and sits on the editorial board of the *Journal of Mental Health Law* (of which he is also an assistant editor). He is the author of *The Nearest Relative Handbook* (Jessica Kingsley Publishers), the second edition of which was recently nominated in the BMA Book Awards, and of a book of essays, *A Tendency to Laugh and Sing: Some Notes on Mental Health Law* (Northumbria Law Press). For nine years, David was a legal member of the Mental Health Act Commission, and he is now a Judge of the First-Tier Tribunal.

Stephen Kirkpatrick is a member of the Chartered Management Institute and has been the Chief Executive of Gold Hill Care, Chalfont St Peter, Buckinghamshire since 2006. Gold Hill Care is a charity which provides residential dementia care for 38 older people, homecare for over 100 adults in the local community, and sheltered accommodation to 12 older people. Prior to this Steve was a Detective Inspector in the Thames Valley Police retiring after completing 30 years service. During his service with the police, Steve worked on several multi-agency committees and on numerous investigations, safeguarding and protecting vulnerable adults. He also served for seven years on the Major Crime Units at Reading and Maidenhead, successfully completing all five modules of the National Crime Faculty accredited Seniors Investigating Officers' Development Programme in 2002.

Geraldine Monaghan is a qualified, General Social Care Council (GSCC) registered social worker who has 30 years experience working in local authority social work. She has worked extensively with children and families and latterly vulnerable adults. She has a good deal of court experience and considerable experience of major joint (police/social services) investigations, where her role has been to manage the social work input. Geraldine is currently the Investigations Manager in the Investigations Support Unit (ISU), a small unit within Liverpool's Community Safety Service, which works closely with police and other partners to support investigations into the abuse of both vulnerable adults and children, when that abuse has forensic elements which lie outside mainstream safeguarding procedures. The unit provides witness support before and during any court proceedings arising from investigation. Geraldine together with Mark Pathak has developed the 'Liverpool Model of Witness Support, Preparation and Profiling'.

Roger Vickers served 30 years with South Yorkshire Police largely in CID retiring in 2002 in the rank of Chief Superintendent. He represented the police on the Sheffield Adult Protection Committee between 1995 and 2002. He was appointed as temporary Independent Chair of the Adult Protection Committee during 2002 and was later confirmed as the Independent Chair of the Sheffield Adult Safeguarding Board, retiring from this post in 2008. Roger has been the independent chair/report writer for eight serious case reviews, one of which produced a recommendation which led to a change in the law on homicide. Roger now works as an Independent Adult Safeguarding Consultant.

Literacy skills

It is important to acknowledge at the very beginning of a book on recording skills that many people struggle with literacy skills and some find it hard to admit that they do have problems. This may be because they fear people seeing them as being 'stupid' or incompetent. Sometimes a person has struggled to learn to read or write when they were a child and subsequently have a block about writing documents. Others may have difficulties which have not been formally diagnosed, for example dyslexia. Even though dyslexia was diagnosed as far back as 1896 it is only in the past 25 years that it has been recognised more widely. We now know that approximately 10 per cent of the population are affected by dyslexia to some degree and that 4 per cent have it severely. About 300,000 of these are children in schools, meaning there is an average of at least one dyslexic child in every classroom (for more information about prevalence see www.bdadyslexia.org.uk and www.literacytrust.org.uk).

It is important to encourage workers to be honest with their managers if they do have any literacy problems and for managers to provide help and support. We are not saying that everyone who has literacy problems will be dyslexic; many workers just need some basic support to assist them in developing literacy skills which they may have failed to do in the past – possibly because no-one had the time or patience to help them.

How much do you know?

The following questionnaire is not meant as test; its purpose is to get the reader thinking about how much they know with regard to recording generally but also relating to specific issues in safeguarding adults work. For the 'no' and 'not sure' responses this book should provide the answers. We suggest that the reader undertakes the questionnaire before starting to read the book and completes it again when they have finished using the book.

The questionnaire could also be used by managers to gauge how confident a worker is regarding their recording skills.

QUESTIONNAIRE

Please answer these questions honestly:

Do you:

1. Know if your organisation has a recording policy and where to access it?

    YES ☐   NO ☐   DON'T KNOW ☐

2. Know *what* your organisation expects you to record?

    YES ☐   NO ☐   DON'T KNOW ☐

3. Know *how* your organisation expects you to record?

    YES ☐   NO ☐   DON'T KNOW ☐

4. Feel confident about your recording skills in general?

    YES ☐   NO ☐   DON'T KNOW ☐

5. Feel you know a sufficient amount about recording in safeguarding adults work?

    YES ☐   NO ☐   DON'T KNOW ☐

6. Know what a noun, adjective and verb are?

    YES ☐   NO ☐   DON'T KNOW ☐

7. Know when to use a comma, semi-colon, colon, quotation mark?

    YES ☐   NO ☐   DON'T KNOW ☐

8. Know the difference between the first and the third person?

    YES ☐   NO ☐   DON'T KNOW ☐

9. Understand the difference between a process record and a running record?

    YES ☐   NO ☐   DON'T KNOW ☐

10. Know what contemporaneous notes are and how long they should be kept?

    YES ☐   NO ☐   DON'T KNOW ☐

11. Understand what constitutes evidence?
    YES ☐   NO ☐   DON'T KNOW ☐

12. Know which written records can be used as evidence?
    YES ☐   NO ☐   DON'T KNOW ☐

13. Know when and how to complete a bodymap?
    YES ☐   NO ☐   DON'T KNOW ☐

14. Understand about archiving documents?
    YES ☐   NO ☐   DON'T KNOW ☐

15. Consistently keep your written notes/messages?
    YES ☐   NO ☐   DON'T KNOW ☐

16. Know who can access your records?
    YES ☐   NO ☐   DON'T KNOW ☐

17. Feel confident about when and how to share information?
    YES ☐   NO ☐   DON'T KNOW ☐

18. Know if your organisation has an information sharing protocol?
    YES ☐   NO ☐   DON'T KNOW ☐

19. Know how to write a report for a case conference?
    YES ☐   NO ☐   DON'T KNOW ☐

20. Know what should be written in a report for court?
    YES ☐   NO ☐   DON'T KNOW ☐

Chapter 2

The Purpose of Keeping Records

Nearly everyone moans about the amount of paperwork that has to be done nowadays and it does seem ever increasing. Many workers find it a chore because they feel they would rather be 'getting on with the real work'; others maybe fearful of having to write because of bad experiences they may have had at school and that stays with them. Unfortunately, in many circumstances no-one has ever explained to a worker *why* written records are so important. A manager may have said countless times it is important to get the recording done and wonderful phrases are repeated frequently, for example 'if it is not written down it hasn't happened.' However, rarely has it been explained how records can be used and the consequences of not recording. Once a worker understands why written records are so important they might put more effort into making their records better. This chapter will explain the purpose in keeping records and take workers beyond 'you record because you have to.' But what does the word 'purpose' actually mean?

DEFINITIONS OF PURPOSE

- *the reason for which something is done or for which something exists*
- *resolve or determination*

(Oxford English Dictionary)

- *reason; point; rationale; function; aim; intention; drive; use.*

(Oxford Concise Thesaurus)

Legal purposes/evidence

Any record kept by an organisation could be used in a court of law if it is thought to be some form of evidence (Chapters 6 will discuss further the different types of written records). Many cases of abuse do not reach court because written records are poor and do not pass the evidential test which has to be carried out by the Crown Prosecution Service (CPS). Michael Mandelstam makes a point regarding local authorities which is actually pertinent to all organisations:

> Good record-keeping is an essential consideration for local authorities, so that, when they are challenged – as is increasingly likely – they are able to demonstrate that decisions were not taken unlawfully or with maladministration. (Mandelstam 1998, p.163)

However, it is not just local authorities that may be challenged regarding their decision-making; all organisations can be scrutinised when an inquiry or serious case review is being undertaken. Organisations and their workers need to consider whether they have a duty of care in the work they do and during the course of the services they provide. Workers also need to be aware under which statutes they are functioning and be clear about which policies and procedures exist and they are expected to implement and follow. One of our expert police officers warns us:

Expert's experience and comment
Far too many professionals delude themselves that failure of their duty will not bring the potential of criminal penalty.

Police Officer

Records as evidence

People say that few cases of adult abuse get to court; this is true but cases do get to court and a lot more would get there if written records were of a higher standard, that is, meet the evidential requirements of the courts. Workers should not become paranoid about the fact that they might have to give evidence in court, but they should strive to write records in a way that will be helpful to anyone who is involved in an abuse investigation. For example, some small change in behaviour that a care worker noticed in a service user could be helpful in proving that abuse was already taking place a long time before the investigation started. It is important that all workers are encouraged to record any change in behaviour, attitude, mood, lifestyle, etc. – no matter how small or trivial it may seem at the time. Workers also need to know what to record when receiving a disclosure about abuse (which often comes out of the blue) and the importance of keeping contemporaneous notes, that is, notes taken at the time of the disclosure (this will be discussed in depth in Chapter 7).

Accountability

Every worker is accountable to the organisation which employs them. Management has to be safe in the knowledge that a worker is doing the job properly; this involves ensuring that the worker is implementing the relevant policies when required and that procedures are being followed correctly. This is achieved by a worker being supervised by a line manager who provides regular supervision sessions. As with the issue of recording, some workers do not like supervision sessions and do everything to avoid them. A manager should provide supervision sessions which cover the four functions of supervision (i.e. management, support, education, mediation), but which are also enjoyable and worthwhile for the worker. Sessions should not be focused solely on workload management and 'number crunching' (as many workers call it). An essential and integral part of supervision is to look at written records. Managers and workers alike constantly talk about increasing workloads and the lack of time to do essential tasks. A manager *must* make time to read a worker's written records; if they do not do this how will the manager know whether a worker is recording properly or be able to give constructive feedback if that is required? Most supervision policies state that a manager should look at a certain number of case files, that is, undertake an audit before each supervision session.

Another important reason for looking at a worker's records is to ensure that gaps in services are being identified; this is a requirement for local authorities under the *NHS and Community Care Act 1990*. When needs are not being met this should be recorded in a service user's file. However, it is also important to raise such issues at strategy meetings and case conferences, and to ensure that it is recorded in the minutes that needs have been highlighted and may not have been met. We are living in an era where workers do have to cover their own backs.

Case example

A case conference was being convened on Mrs King, a 77-year-old woman who lives in a care home and is confused. Mrs King has a history of manic depression. She had been a victim of indecent assault, the perpetrator being another resident. Mrs King's social worker had worked closely with the police during the investigation and had recommended to the case conference that Mrs King would benefit from therapy sessions from a local psychotherapist who specialises in this area of work. After discussion it was concluded that there was no funding for this type of therapy and it was agreed that a community psychiatric nurse would provide three counselling sessions. The social worker said Mrs King needed specialised therapy not general counselling and requested it was minuted that, 'in my view we are not meeting Mrs King's needs.' After the conference the social worker wrote on Mrs King's file that she was not happy with the outcome of the conference because 'specialist resources to address the long-term effects of the abuse Mrs King has experienced have not been provided and in my opinion this is detrimental to Mrs King's well-being and recovery from abuse.'

Justifying actions and decision-making

Being accountable means that workers have to justify their actions; they cannot act alone – there is a need to explain why they are working in a certain way. This is important for an individual worker but also for organisations as a whole. The Department of Health guidance *No Secrets* (DH 2000) has always promoted inter-agency working, whereas the national framework of standards *Safeguarding Adults* (ADSS 2005) talks about working in partnership. Working with abuse cases necessitates joint decision-making.

A record should not just state the fact; there also needs to be an explanation regarding the reasons and logic behind the decision-making and action. Workers can come under scrutiny in many different circumstances: for example, a complaint is lodged; an inquiry or serious case review is undertaken; an individual or organisation is sued. There will be times when these things occur a long time after a record has actually been written. So this begs the question:

> **KEY QUESTION**
>
> • Are your written records good enough to trigger your memory about why you made a decision or took a specific action?

Therefore, just writing down the action may not be enough. The content of the record needs to be written in a way that means it can act as an aide-memoire – maybe years later!

BEST PRACTICE POINTS

• A record should explain what you did and why you did it.
• When decisions are made, the reasons for making a decision should be explained.

Safeguard against allegations

Unfortunately we are living in a world where workers have to cover their own backs; this being due mainly to the fact that we live in a society where a 'blame culture' has become the norm and the amount of litigation is on the increase. This should not be the main reason why recording is important, but it reiterates the point made above that workers must be able to recall what they did and the reasons behind their action(s). Recording is a real safeguard if somebody accuses a worker of doing something or not doing something. A record should be written in a way that will help a care worker remember the sequence of events but also exactly what happened and why.

Written records as a form of communication

A worker can talk verbally in supervision about what work they have undertaken with a service user, but it is equally important to use different types of records to actually explain the methods of working. Recording is a form of communication. It has been evident in past and recent child abuse inquiries[1] that communication between agencies has been poor, so it is necessary to look at all the different ways workers can communicate which includes written records. Key words or phrases which regularly occur in all child abuse inquiries are: 'poor communication'; 'poor quality information'; 'inadequate client information'. Hence, the reason why organisations must consider how and when to share information and develop appropriate protocols to achieve this (see the following chapter for further discussion).

A written record is a way of communicating:

- what work is being undertaken (objectives)

- how work is being done (methods)

- explanation regarding what work has been done (monitor, review, evaluate)

- needs

- incidents/events

- opinions

- reasons underpinning decision-making.

Who records are written for

When starting to write a certain document, the author might know who the potential readership is, but in other circumstances the potential audience may not be known (or even considered) or circumstances could change in the future so that a wider audience has access to the record. So key questions to begin with are:

KEY QUESTIONS

- Who am I writing the record for?
- Who else might need to read the record in the future?

---

1   There have been numerous inquiries over the years. A useful overview can be found in Reder *et al.* (1993) *Beyond Blame: Child Abuse Tragedies Revisited*; particularly Chapter 6 'Inter-professional communication'. More recently the Laming reports regarding the deaths of Victoria Climbié (2003) and Peter Connelly (2009).

A worker will alter their style of writing depending on what sort of document they are writing and for whom they are writing it. The content and layout will differ depending on the intended outcome which is to be achieved. A written document conveys information and will seek to achieve something, namely, to inform the reader. A care worker in a residential home writing in a communications book will write in a very different style to a social worker who writes an application which is going to go to a resource panel; and this will differ again from a probation officer who is writing a report to be heard in a court. Even the way notes are written will differ between workers – a nurse writing notes in medical records will be different from a home care worker writing notes on a file kept in a service user's home.

There could be all sorts of different circumstances that arise when working with abuse in which people may need or have the right to read a record (strategy meeting, abuse investigation, case conference, public/coroner's inquiry, serious case review, judicial review). Therefore, what follows are some possible answers to the questions, but the list is not exhaustive:

- the author of the record and line manager
- professionals/workers in the same organisation
- professionals/workers from other organisations, for example care providers, police, solicitors, barristers, defence lawyers, coroner, personnel within the Care Quality Commission, Crown Prosecution Service, etc.
- service user.

The exercise opposite is useful for a worker to undertake in order to think about access and readership to their records.

Involving the service user

We must not forget the service user. Empowerment is talked about a great deal nowadays and enabling a service user to contribute to his or her own written record can be empowering. Some victims of abuse do write about the abuse they experience just after the event; such writing could be used as evidence. This will be explored further in Chapter 6, but it is useful to remind the reader that older people often kept diaries in years gone by. Many older victims of abuse have recorded what happened to them in such diaries. Younger and older adults may also use creative writing (e.g. poetry) to record what has happened to them. It is also important to be mindful of the fact that any worker should be working in an open way with their service users and that a service user has not only the right to contribute to their record but the right to apply to see their records.

EXERCISE 2.1

WHO MIGHT READ YOUR RECORDING?

OBJECTIVE
To encourage a worker to think about who might read their written records.

PARTICIPANTS
Individual.

EQUIPMENT
Paper and pen; work diary.

TIME
10 minutes.

TASK
1. Have your diary with you and on an A4 sheet put a line down the middle to create two columns.
2. Open your diary and look at your work activities for the last week. As you are reading through make a list of all the types of written documents you wrote for work purposes in the left hand column (this should include any notes taken during an event or which you made afterwards). Number each type of document you write down and leave some space between each one.
3. When the list is complete, read it again. In the right hand column list all the potential people who might have a reason to read that document in the near or distant future.

FEEDBACK
Keep this A4 sheet and read it again in 3, 6 and 12 months time. When you know one of the documents has been read by someone you put on the list put a tick. If someone else accesses the document who you had not thought of when undertaking the exercise add them to the list.

Methodology

What is often missing in many records is an explanation of what methods a worker is using in their day-to-day practice. Professionals and workers develop skills, knowledge and expertise so it all becomes second nature; they then find it difficult to state what is obvious to them. It is important that should a worker leave a job or go off on long-term sick leave unexpectedly then his or her records should be good enough for a manager or another worker to pick up where the previous worker left off. That is to say not only should the service user's details be there but the methods utilised to work with that person should be explained.

In safeguarding adults cases which reach court, a worker's practice and ways of working may also be questioned. Therefore, good recording should include detail about:

- methodology
- problem solving
- planning for future work.

Reflection and evaluation

A sound committed worker will want to do their best for service users and to achieve this there must be reflection on what has been done and what has been achieved. Evaluating work practices openly and honestly is the key to best practice. This can be undertaken in supervision sessions and as discussed already it is important that managers read their workers' files in order to achieve this through reflective practice. It is not good enough to say 'there is not enough time to do this'; this could lead to dangerous practice. It is also important that managers write on service users' files to reflect their views or to state reasons why methodology might be changing. With the current pressures of work, managers might not take the time to do this, but it should be part of the management and supervision process.

Learning and objectivity

Looking back through records can facilitate learning and objectivity. A worker should take time to read back through a file if other workers have been involved previously, but it is equally important for a worker to read through their own recordings. When a service user has been

EXERCISE 2.2

HOW GOOD IS MY RECORDING?

OBJECTIVE
To reflect back on old written records and consider how they could be produced in a better way.

PARTICIPANTS
Individual.

EQUIPMENT
Paper and pen; service user records.

TIME
This will depend on how many old records can be accessed.

TASK

1. Try to find some examples of records you have written in the past. If possible it is helpful for the purpose of this exercise to obtain records which have been written over an extensive period of time, not just going back a few months or a year. It is also good if you can collect a number of different types of recordings (e.g. service files; notes taken; assessments; review forms; letters; e-mails).

2. Read through all the documents you have collected in one sitting.

3. Then focus on one document at a time. Ask yourself the following questions:

    a. Is this a good written record?

    b. How could it be improved?

    c. Would you write anything differently?

FEEDBACK
Once you have gone through each document spend some time reflecting on:

1. What has been good and bad about your recording in the past?

2. Has your recording style changed in any way in the period of time under consideration?

3. Is there anything you need to do differently now?

4. What have you learnt from doing this exercise?

known to a worker for a while it is easy to forget about things that have happened in the past or how situations were some time ago. This leads back to reflecting again but also enabling a worker to learn from what has worked (success) and what has not worked (failure), that is, they can learn and also be objective.

Risk assessment and risk management

Taking risks is a part of everybody's life and in the work situation workers are encouraged not to be 'risk-averse'. Another phrase we hear a lot is he or she 'is at risk'. At risk of what exactly? Most people mean 'harm' but again risk assessments need to be explicit. Risk assessments are an integral part of working with cases where there are suspicions or allegations about abuse. As early as the alert stage a worker should be asking certain questions: 'Is the service user safe at this moment in time'; 'Could he or she be harmed in the future?' Sometimes it is impossible to answer these questions because very little information is available at this stage, but a risk assessment should be part of the referral process and considered in a strategy meeting, where an interim safeguarding plan could be developed. The risk assessment continues as an investigation progresses and should be part of the case conference agenda. Once a formal safeguarding plan is agreed the risk management stage has been reached. Both risk assessment and risk management through a safeguarding plan will be discussed fully in Chapter 9. However, it is important to say here that any conflict in opinion regarding the level of risk should always be written down not just discussed verbally. This is why any risk tool should include a 'conflict box'.

Monitoring and reviewing

The word 'monitor' is heard a lot in many work situations and in some ways is a bit of a cliché. Workers may say, 'I'll monitor the situation for a while' or 'X goes in regularly so they can monitor' – but what and how are these people monitoring? When a person or a situation is being monitored the details need to be written down regarding:

- what is being monitored
- by whom
- when and where is the monitoring taking place
- where the findings will be recorded.

In day-to-day work, most workers monitor via a care plan which is reviewed at regular intervals; safeguarding adults cases should be monitored though a safeguarding plan which will be reviewed initially through a case conference. As already stated a safeguarding plan will be developed after a risk assessment has been undertaken.

BEST PRACTICE POINTS

Before you start writing any record think about:
- the purpose
- what information needs to be given to the reader
- what you need to say
- what you are trying to achieve in this written communication
- who might read the record.

Suggested reading

Laming, Lord (2003) *The Victoria Climbié Report*. London: The Stationery Office.

Laming, Lord (2009) *The Protection of Children in England: A Progress Report*. London: The Stationery Office.

Reder, P. and Duncan S. (1999) *Lost Innocents: A Follow-up Study of Fatal Child Abuse*. London: Routledge.

Reder, P., Duncan, S. and Gray, M. (1993) *Beyond Blame: Child Abuse Tragedies Revisited*. London: Routledge.

Schon, D.A. (1991) *The Reflective Practitioner: How Professionals Think in Action*. London: Temple Smith.

Thompson, S. and Thompson, N. (2008) *The Critically Reflective Practitioner*. Basingstoke: Palgrave Macmillan.

Chapter 3

Access to Records and Information Sharing

Workers across all the sectors should have a clear understanding regarding who can access a service user's records. Yet when questioned about this, workers can be unclear about what can and cannot be shared. Most workers are familiar with the term 'sharing on a need to know basis' but few can say where this term comes from or explain what it means exactly, that is, what are the criteria for needing to know something? There is often inconsistency in practice; some workers do readily share information, while others automatically block requests for information which actually are justified or legitimate. This chapter will address some of the key issues regarding access.

There has been a deluge of legislation and case law regarding the sharing of personal information in the last decade. In this chapter we shall discuss the legal rules which are relevant to case recording, service users' records and obtaining evidence to prove that abuse has happened. This chapter is not meant to be a comprehensive guide to each statute; the reader will be signposted to helpful references.

Service users' understanding of records

Another concern is that service users may not be clear about what types of information are recorded on their file and who might have access to it. Workers need to spend time explaining in detail why and how files are kept. There is a tendency for workers to talk in generalised terms rather than giving the service user detailed information. All workers should ponder on whether a service user really understands:

- what type of records are kept (paper file or electronic record)
- where they are kept (office, home of worker, computer, filing cabinet)
- who can write on the record (e.g. worker, manager, others)

- who can access/read the record (e.g. other members of the team, administrative workers, other people in the organisation or outside it)

- that a service user has the right to contribute to their own record

- that a service user has the right to apply to read their own record.

It needs to be borne in mind that every service user is going to have different life experience and cognitive ability to understand records. For example, some older people may never have physically sat in front of a computer and have only seen how they might work whilst watching a television programme. Other service users may not know who else works alongside their own worker; they cannot imagine the location of the office or how things work. Nowadays more people are working from home; does the service user know this? Neither might they realise just how many forms have to be completed in any workplace nowadays – either on paper or electronically. Therefore, things which are commonplace for a worker because it is all part of their work practices, might not be so easily understood by a service user if they have not had certain experiences. This is why clear explanations should be given by a worker when first meeting a service user; and these issues should be revisited on a regular basis.

BEST PRACTICE POINTS

- Workers need to explain clearly what confidentiality means in the working relationship and the limits to confidentiality, that is, a worker cannot keep secrets.
- Service users need to understand when and how a worker may have to share information, namely, over-ride self-determination and break confidentiality.
- A service user should be aware of what records are kept and who can access them.

The word 'confidentiality'

We need to have some discussion regarding confidentiality. The word 'confidentiality' means different things to different people and can result in a great deal of confusion. A lay person may think its meaning is as is stated in various dictionary definitions:

DEFINITIONS OF CONFIDENTIAL

- *spoken, written, acted on etc., in strict privacy or secrecy; secret*
- *indicating confidence or intimacy; imparting private matters*
- *having another's trust confidence; entrusted with secrets or private affairs*

(Dictionary.com undated)

- *intended to be kept secret*
- *entrusted with private information.*

(Oxford English Dictionary)

The courts have defined confidential information as information which is available to one person, or a group who do not intend it to become generally available. The person supplying the information does not need to specify that it is confidential. Usually the relationship between the people involved will be enough to make information exchanged between them confidential, for example doctor and patient, social worker and client. Sometimes it will be obvious from the situation, or from what is said that the information is intended to be treated as confidential. This is sometimes referred to as a duty of confidence.

The exercise opposite can be helpful in getting a worker to think about what the term confidentiality means in their own work role.

In a lot of definitions the word 'secret' comes up and in a working relationship it needs to be made clear that a worker cannot keep secrets. Therefore, it has to be made explicit that in a work situation the definition can be different; if a worker has not given a clear explanation about this at the beginning of a working relationship then a lot of confusion and misunderstanding can occur. It is vital that any worker spends time explaining the meaning of confidentiality, but also the limits to confidentiality within the relationship.

The service user needs to understand that any information given to a worker belongs to the organisation which employs them, not to the individual worker. A worker has to make it clear that their role is not like that of a priest, who listens to confession and keeps it secret. It should also be stressed that where there is concern that the service user or other people could be harmed then it will be necessary to share this 'on a need to know basis'. So where did this phrase come from? It dates back to

EXERCISE 3.1

DEFINING CONFIDENTIALITY

OBJECTIVE
To make workers think about what confidentiality means to them in their work role.

PARTICIPANTS
To work individually and then in a large group.

EQUIPMENT
Trainer to give each participant half a sheet of A4 paper.

TIME
5 minutes to write definition.
20 minutes group discussion.

TASK

1. Think about what confidentiality means to you in your work role.

2. Write a definition of confidentiality: 'Confidentiality is...' on the piece of paper which has been given to you.

3. Fold the piece of paper in half and half again. Throw it into the middle of the floor.

4. Trainer collects pieces of paper, shuffles them and then gives one piece of paper to each participant.

5. In turn each participant reads out the definition on the piece of paper they have been given and then pauses. Participants are asked to comment on the definition which has been read out.

NOTE FOR TRAINER
It is important to make this exercise very safe. When explaining the exercise to participants you must ensure the following:

1. A ground rule should be put in place that the author of the definition will not be identified so that people will speak freely.

2. If someone gets their own definition back or they recognise someone's handwriting, they should not say so.

3. Participants can ask for the definition to be read out again.

when the Department of Health defined the principles of confidentiality as follows:

- Information should be used only for the purposes for which it was given.

- Information about a user/patient should normally be shared only with the consent of that person.

- Information should be shared on a 'need to know' basis.

- Users and carers should be advised why and with whom information concerning them has been shared.

- All confidential information should be rigorously safeguarded.

(Department of Health 1991, p.34)

Safeguarding adults and sharing information

So far we have been talking generally about the limits of confidentiality and sharing information in a worker's day-to-day work. It is now important that we relate this to safeguarding adults work. Information can be shared verbally or in written format; the remit of this book is to focus on recording and therefore we are considering the latter format. The DH guidance *No Secrets* emphasises working in an inter-agency way; the ADSS framework of standards *Safeguarding Adults* uses the term 'working in partnership'. So organisations and their workers are being encouraged to share information in order to protect an adult who may be at risk of abuse, namely harm, but they also have to be mindful of the adult's human rights, which necessitates having some knowledge of the Articles of the European Convention on Human Rights (ECHR). Three Articles which are particularly pertinent to safeguarding adults are:

Article 2: Right to life.

Article 3: Right not to be subjected to torture, or inhuman or degrading treatment.

Article 8: Right to respect for private and family life.

If a worker feels they are not familiar with the European Convention on Human Rights or the *Human Rights Act 1998* or they have not attended a training course to be updated on the Act in recent years then it is useful to get a copy of *A Guide to the Human Rights Act 1998* which is published by the Department for Constitutional Affairs (2006). This guide explains the articles in very simple language, but also poses frequently asked questions and presents simple explanations. Here is a brief example regarding Article 8, which may be relevant to some abuse situations:

> **3.68** You have the right to respect for your private and family life, your home and your correspondence. Article 8 is an example of a qualified right in the ECHR. This means that there is a framework in place against which any interference with your rights by the state must be judged to see if it is acceptable.

> ### What does private life cover?
> **3.69** The concept of 'private life' is broad. In general, your right to a private life means that you have the right to live your own life with such personal privacy as is reasonable in a democratic society, taking into account the rights and freedoms of others. Any interference with your body or the way you live your life needs to be justified. Your Article 8 rights include matters of self-determination that may include, for example:

> - freedom to choose your sexual identity
> - freedom to choose how you look and dress
> - freedom from intrusion by the media.

> **3.70** Your right to private life can also include the right to have information about you, such as official records, photographs, letters, diaries and medical information, kept private and confidential. Unless there is a very good reason, public authorities should not collect or use information like this; if they do, they need to make sure the information is accurate.

> **3.71** Article 8 places limits on the extent to which a public authority can do things which invade your privacy about your body without your permission. This can include activities such as taking blood samples and performing body searches.

> **3.72** In some circumstances, the state must take positive steps to prevent intrusions into your privacy by other people. For example, the state may be required to take action to protect individuals from serious pollution where it is seriously affecting their lives.

> (DCA 2006, p.21)

Any worker or their organisation has to justify their actions; if self-determination is to be over-ridden or confidentiality broken then it must be recorded on the service user's file, that is, the logic behind the decision to do this and where possible to state under which statute the worker is acting (e.g. Section 115, *Crime and Disorder Act 1998* – to be discussed below). It is very important to record and explain the risk assessment (or any other reason for over-riding someone's rights), and to show that sharing information is justified and a proportionate step. Information can be shared in certain circumstances; it is useful to take another example from the DCA Study Guide:

> **Can a public authority interfere with my Article 8 rights?**
>
> **3.76** Yes. But it would have to be shown that: the interference had a clear legal basis; the *aim* of the interference was either national security, public safety, protection of the economy, prevention of crime, the protection of health or morals or the protection of the rights and freedoms of others; it was necessary (and not just reasonable) to interfere with your rights for one of the permitted reasons; and that the interference was proportionate, going only as far as was required to meet the aim.
>
> **3.77** Before taking decisions affecting people's rights under Article 8, a public authority will have to weigh all the competing interests carefully so as to justify any interference. Rights under Article 8 may need to be balanced against other rights, for example the right to free expression in Article 10.
>
> (DCA 2006, p.22)

It is now necessary to consider some legal rules which have relevance for sharing information in relation to safeguarding adults work and abuse investigations.

Consent to share information

A worker who is considering sharing confidential information needs to be clear whether they have the consent of the person concerned. Ideally consent should always be in a written format and not just given verbally. Many consent forms are open-ended and the service user may be oblivious to what they are actually consenting to; when information is shared with certain individuals the service user may then object. Therefore consent forms should be explicit about the individuals and agencies the information may be shared with, and the reasons for sharing it. The form should also make clear how long the consent is to last. Workers should explain clearly who they might want to communicate with, although obviously not every circumstance can be envisaged.

Agencies and workers need to bear in mind that some people may not have the mental capacity to agree to information about them being shared. If someone lacks this capacity, they should not be asked to sign to say they agree to their information being shared. In fact, anything they did sign would be legally invalid. If they are assessed not to have this capacity, this should be carefully recorded. It will be for the holder of the information to decide whether to disclose it. This will be on the basis that disclosure would be in the person's best interests, or for some other over-riding reason (for example the duty to assist the police investigating a serious crime.)

KEY QUESTIONS

- Has the service user consented to my disclosing this information to this person/agency?
- Was the consent given orally? (If so, how was it recorded?)
- Do I need to check their capacity to consent?
- If they lack capacity to consent, am I satisfied that this disclosure is in their best interests? (Who will be helped to avert risk, and how?)
- Is this disclosure supported by either informed consent or some other over-riding reason?

Expert's experience and comment

Assessment of capacity is often based on ignorance. It is useless a person saying someone is 'non compos mentis' – based on ignorance – the details are missing. They should have a list of questions that have been asked and the answers. They should note down the interpretation of the answers. Question: 'What would you do if won £10,000 when you went to the bookies?' Good response: 'Seek advice from the bank manager.' Bad answer: 'Stick it in the freezer to hide it from the Martians.' It is a question of detail. The Mini Mental Test[1] is OK to be done BUT not totally helpful in assessing capacity. It is not enough.

---

1   Clinicians and other professionals may know this as the Mini-Mental State Examination, 'the most commonly used instrument for screening cognitive function' (Thomas 2010).

We need individual detail. The greater the magnitude of the decision, the more detail is required.

Niall Baker, lawyer

Organisations develop consent forms for different purposes, but many of them are very vague and non-specific. It is important to be specific because a person may agree to some information being shared with particular people but not with others; or there may be particular subjects which cannot be shared at all. It is important that in-depth conversations take place to ascertain the wishes and agreement of the service user.

BEST PRACTICE POINTS

A consent form should include the following:
Details of service user, i.e. name, date of birth, address.
Statements regarding the following:
- **agreement** about information which can be shared:
  - listing particular topics/subject areas/issues
  - who this information can be shared with – stating name, organisation, relationship
  - in what circumstances the information can be shared (e.g. single assessment, abuse investigation, a medical emergency)
- **restrictions** regarding information which cannot be shared:
  - listing particular topics/subject areas/issues
  - who specifically cannot have access to information if it can be shared with some and not others
- **explanations** have been given and understood regarding:
  - confidentiality (what it means, its limits and circumstances in which it may have to be broken)
  - storage of information (paper files; electronic records; Data Protection Act 1998)
  - access to records (who within the organisation has access; when people from other agencies may have the right to access)
- **timescales:** regarding validity of consent or review date
- **declaration of consent:** print name of service user; signature
- **witness:** print name of worker; job title; signature; details of anyone else present and signature
- **date and time.**

It is important to utilise certain phrases within a consent form, for example, I agree; I disagree; I understand; I consent to; I do not give consent to, etc. Some safeguarding adults policies have specific consent forms which are used during an abuse investigation and are designed so that a worker can state when they are over-riding self-determination and breaking confidentiality. In the following example an older man who has various health problems including emphysema disclosed to his social worker that his son had physically abused him.

Case example

I do not agree to:

The police being told the things I have told Jenny today.

Signature: Adam Beresford   Date: 6 April 2010

Decision to share information:

Mr Beresford told me during my visit this morning (10.05–11.00) that his son had cut him with a pen knife after threatening to 'hurt' him if he did not give him £300 to pay his credit card bill. Mr Beresford showed me his right hand, which had several lacerations on the palm. He also showed me one long (approximately 15 centimetres) cut on his left lower arm. He refused medical treatment. Mr Beresford disclosed that his son is 'drinking excessively every day' and that he is 'very frightened of him'. After discussion with my team manager at 12.15, we agreed that the police should be informed as I have assessed Mr Beresford to be at risk of further harm. Therefore, I shall be sharing my concerns with the Police. I have the power to do this under Section 115 of the Crime and Disorder Act 1998 as I believe a physical assault has taken place and could occur again.

Worker (signed): J. Barton

Jennifer Barton, Social Worker

Date: 6.4.10   Time: 13.30

Expert's experience and comment

Capacity is a presumption and its link to the rights of privacy and self-determination are important for personal liberty. However, I feel sometimes in safeguarding, the police and other professionals can be too quick to close an investigation on the say so of the vulnerable adult deemed to have capacity. When that person is suffering or likely to suffer significant harm and exploitation, is obeying their wish always a defensible position?

By definition being vulnerable is hardly a position of strength, and effectively consenting to suffer significant harm is more than about making poor choices and decisions. The current situation puts me in mind of the dark days of domestic abuse when the police always took a victim's 'no' for an answer and left many to suffer terrible crimes.

These days the professional response to domestic abuse is increasingly enlightened. The starting point of any investigation is to presume victim co-operation and consent may not be forthcoming. These victims have 'capacity' yet the investigation should not stop even in the face of outright hostility. It proceeds in a way that does not rely on the victim, yet should be dedicated to maximising their welfare and safety through timely and robust multi-agency action. This absolute duty of care is expressed through enhanced investigation, working together across the agencies of welfare and justice, and dynamic risk assessment. There should be no negative position in the investigation of domestic abuse.

In my own experience where the circumstances allow I have used Police Domestic Abuse policy in primacy over Adult Abuse Procedures for the simple reasons that the response is more immediate and effective in protecting the vulnerable adult. The crucial factor is its positive arrest requirement with an officer having to justify why none was made. For example, the 90-year-old with bruising (and capacity) alleged to have been the result of a punch by her 50-year-old son does not have to give her consent to the police investigating such a serious crime. The son was arrested at the scene and quickly brought the attention of the relevant agencies into sharp focus.

There seem to be many parallels between domestic abuse and the safeguarding of vulnerable adults, yet the policy of the latter seems years behind.

Police Officer

Sharing information protocols

Over the years sharing information protocols have developed between agencies. Such protocols are agreements between agencies about how and when information should be shared. The DH recommended development of such protocols in *No Secrets:*

> **5.5 Confidentiality.** Agencies should draw up a common agreement relating to confidentiality and setting out the principles governing the sharing of information based on the best interests of the vulnerable adult. In doing so they will need to distinguish between the principles of confidentiality designed to safeguard the best interests of the service user and those protecting other aspects of management. (DH 2000, p.24)

Seven years later the Commission for Social Care Inspection (now the Care Quality Commission) produced *Safeguarding Adults Protocols and Guidance* which was 'formally agreed with the Association of Directors of Social Services (ADSS) and Association of Chief Police Officers (ACPO). The protocol has the support of the Department of Health. Any regional or local agreements in place must be compatible with this national protocol' (CSCI 2007, p.2).

The ADSS document *Safeguarding Adults* also addresses the importance of information-sharing protocols in Standard 6:

> **6.12** There is an information-sharing protocol between partner agencies, and those contracted to provided services by them, that covers all aspects of 'Safeguarding Adults' work. This includes the rights of adults to access data about them.

> **6.13** The information-sharing protocol includes the rights of an alleged perpetrator to know the nature of the concerns about their behaviour, to have a right of reply and have an opportunity to correct any information held about them that is not accurate. (ADSS 2005, p.24)

Where Safeguarding Adults policies do not have a specific sharing information protocol within them agencies may rely on a local sharing information protocol which has been developed under the *Crime and Disorder Act 1998*. It was a requirement under the Act that every area in the UK should develop such a protocol in order to reduce crime in the local area. Section 115 of the Act is known as the 'sharing information principle', which will cover a number of safeguarding situations but is not a general power to disclose, especially where the abuse does not amount to a criminal offence.

Sharing information in abuse cases
Section 115 Crime and Disorder Act 1998

When dealing with cases of abuse it will be necessary to share information and it is important that an alleged victim understands this. When a worker shares information with their own line manager they are not breaking confidentiality; this goes back to the point that information belongs to the organisation. An alerter must tell an alleged victim that they are going to report any concerns they have. If it is thought that a crime has been committed a manager may feel that they have to pass the alert on – either to social services or the police. The argument for this is that it may be in the public interest to do this, that is, it is a public protection issue. Under Section 115 of the *Crime and Disorder Act 1998* a worker has the power to share information with personnel in certain agencies (local authority, health authority, probation, police) if it is thought a crime has been committed or could be committed in the future.

Domestic Violence, Crime and Victims Act 2004

This is another very important Act which can create a duty to protect children and vulnerable adults, including by sharing information with the police or local authority. Section 5 of the Domestic Violence Crime and Victims Act 2004 applies if a child or vulnerable adult is being subjected to or is witnessing domestic violence. If the child or vulnerable adult later dies and was at significant risk of serious harm, people living in the household can be prosecuted if they failed to take reasonable steps to protect the victim. The same applies to anyone who visited the household frequently and for long enough to be regarded as a member of the household.

So live-in carers, and those who spend significant time looking after a child or vulnerable adult should record very carefully any incidents, comments or behaviour they witness which could suggest that the person they look after is at serious risk. They should write clearly on the service user file that they are acting under Section 5 of the Act, which relates to what is sometimes called 'familial homicide'. Many victims of domestic violence will not want the matter reported and therefore the worker will be over-riding self-determination. In case of doubt about whether (or what) to record, workers should ask for advice. Each recorded incident should be risk assessed to decide if, on its own or taken together with other information it should be reported.

Caldicott Principles, Data Protection Act, Human Rights and Common Law

Any decision to share information without the consent of the source and subject should be based on a careful balancing of:

1. the rights of the source and/or subject to confidentiality at common law, and privacy under Article 8 of the European Convention on Human Rights (ECHR). These rights should be taken to include rights to reputation and livelihood, and the privacy of both one's home and correspondence; and

2. the harm likely to result from not sharing the information.

Whether one looks at the Caldicott Principles, the Data Protection Act, Human Rights or the common law the basic approach is similar. It may be helpful to ask two questions:

KEY QUESTIONS

- Do I have the person's consent to share this information?
- Is there a strong reason to share this information?

First, has the person consented to my sharing this information? They may have signed a consent form when the worker or agency first became involved. It is important to check though that the particular disclosure is covered by any general consent. Would the person have considered this disclosure as covered by the form they signed or is this disclosure really outside its reasonable scope – in which case we need to obtain consent afresh and ensure the person understands the use their information will be put to. We also need to consider whether the person has capacity to agree to their information being shared. If not, any apparent agreement is invalid and should not be requested.

Second, is there a sufficiently strong reason to take the exceptional step of sharing what is highly confidential information? It is important to be clear that there is a compelling reason to share the information. This could be that the risk to them is assessed as significant, and also that sharing it in this way is part of an inter-agency plan to address that risk. The law is clear that information-sharing to avert risk must be based on a risk assessment. The courts have consistently made clear that information should not be shared on an 'in case' basis (in case it may help the recipient address risk) and that the holder of the risk must judge that there is a sufficient risk to justify sharing confidential information.

Apart from risk, there may be other over-riding reasons to disclose information, for example under a legal duty or a court order. Legal advice should also be sought in these cases.

The reason for disclosing information should always be carefully recorded, particularly where consent to disclosure is refused, or for whatever reason we decide not to seek consent. Practitioners should also bear in mind the human right of all adults, including those who are vulnerable to be protected from treatment which is 'inhuman or degrading' (Article 3 ECHR).

How and when information is shared

Workers need to be clear about why information is being shared. In general, this is because – in a safeguarding adults situation – the risk has been assessed as sufficient to over-ride the usual duty of confidentiality. But that general rule is never enough on its own. Workers have to record the specific reasons why the particular information is being disclosed – what is the risk and how is sharing the information designed to help address it.

Many victims of abuse will choose to stay in an abusive situation and may not want other people to know of their plight. Many workers quite rightly promote the principle of self-determination but where a crime has been committed it is necessary to share that information in order to prevent other people being harmed. The key findings of many child protection inquiries and serious case reviews have been that professionals have failed to communicate when children have been at risk of harm.

When a worker does break confidentiality they need to justify this on the service user file, that is, explain the reasons for doing so. This goes back to the recurring theme in this book that a worker should not just write down an action but explain the logic and decision-making behind that action.

Suggested reading

Department for Constitutional Affairs (2006) *A Guide to the Human Rights Act 1998.* 3rd Edition. London: DCA.

Hewitt, D. (2008) 'The vulnerable adult and the Mental Capacity Act 2005.' In J. Pritchard (ed.) *Good Practice in the Law and Safeguarding Adults.* London: Jessica Kingsley Publishers.

Leslie, S. (2008) 'Confidentiality and information sharing.' In J. Pritchard (ed.) *Good Practice in the Law and Safeguarding Adults.* London: Jessica Kingsley Publishers.

Leslie, S. (2008) 'Using the Mental Capacity Act to protect vulnerable adults.' In J. Pritchard (ed.) *Good Practice in Safeguarding Adults.* London: Jessica Kingsley Publishers.

Chapter 4

Back to Basics: Good Recording Skills

This chapter is going to go back to basics because of the concern that was raised at the very beginning of this book, that is, that many workers have never had in-depth training on how to record properly. This chapter will help those workers and then the following chapters will take a more in-depth look at what is required in safeguarding adults work.

There are so many different types of records, yet workers rarely sit down to think about how many there are exactly and how each one could be used in different situations. Statutory agencies rely heavily on computers and can sometimes forget that other organisations are not so well resourced or advanced in the use of technology. Therefore, there are many organisations that still keep paper records or a mixture of both paper and electronic records.

This chapter will be considering the traditional methods of recording on paper records. A worker who may only be using computer records should also benefit from reading this chapter, because it is about promoting best practice in recording skills which can also be applied to any electronic records. Workers often complain on training courses that the computer software does not allow them to record as they wish to do. In those situations, a Word file can always be created, additional recording entered which can then be uploaded. A software package should not hinder a worker's recording. There is also often a fear that management will not like a worker using other tools or protocols. As long as a worker is completing the records required by their organisation (i.e. following policy and procedure) then there is nothing wrong with a worker using additional tools which promote good recording skills.

We shall be going back to basic recording skills in this chapter and at the same time will start to relate this to safeguarding adults work by including comments and advice from experts.

Keeping records and archiving

Every organisation should have a recording policy which clearly sets out what is expected of its workers.

KEY QUESTION

- Do you know if your organisation has a recording policy?

Within that policy there should be guidance regarding the archiving and storage of records. In many adult social care agencies records are kept on average for either 5, 7 or 10 years. Police forces have tended to keep records for 7 years but in recent years some forces have made decisions to keep their records for much longer e.g. 30 years. One police officer who believes in archiving for longer periods of time describes his own practice regarding archiving files related to abuse cases:

Expert's experience and comment

I have kept all handwritten documents/notes and statements taken since coming into post in secure storage. What practitioners from all agencies have to consider is that at present the judicial system in the UK is still reliant on the production of original documents in court cases. For me, this is interpreted as every item of paper written on in relation to cases, no matter how trivial. If an item is scanned, a record is made of who has done this, and the date/time it was done, as well as a trail of where the original is stored. It's important, because say a carer was accused of something but it was not proven. Much later the same style allegation comes up again. We can use what we have stored as bad character evidence in the next case as part of the investigation.

Police Officer

Niall Baker, a lawyer, also keeps things for a long time:

Expert's experience and comment

I write everything down in a book – brief handwritten notes. All notes are subsequently dictated and expanded but I still have the originals. Scanning is fine – contemporaneous notes to be relied upon should be signed and dated. However, if they are in your handwriting, you know you have written them.

They need to be dictated within 2–3 days, not weeks. The key is to log detail. You don't want to give people an opportunity to mount a valid challenge against decisions you have made.

Niall Baker

Steve Kirkpatrick says:

Expert's experience and comment

Since 1990 I have kept records in an A4 hardback book. So conversations of significance would be entered, notes of meetings, even my reflections and my rationale for any decision making and things to do are in these books. If file notes have to be kept, I prefer to type them up from my notes and place them on a file. I have from time to time kept such notes on A4 individual pages and placed them in the file, but this is not so good. The reason being is that it sometimes helps to see other work and pressures we are under when we are dealing with any particular cases. To see other decisions we have had to make. This can sometimes speak volumes of why, for example, we did not notify something until the following day.

Steve Kirkpatrick

Organising records

Every organisation will have its system of recording and expect workers to keep files in a certain way. A key consideration should be whether someone from another agency could find documents easily if they had access to the file (e.g. the police, solicitor in the Crown Prosecution Service). Where specific documents are located should be easily identifiable in paper files; computer software packages should be user-friendly.

If your organisation uses both paper and computerised recording systems, it is vital to ensure that information which is needed for safeguarding is not 'lost' between the two. If you record on paper in the first instance, it is important to make sure that this is transferred to computer promptly and checked for completeness and accuracy. The paper originals of some records likely to be evidentially important should be kept until it is clear that they are no longer required. In general however, it is important to make certain all recorded information is entered into a computerised system if your organisation has one.

For many years recording has involved keeping *running records* and *process records*. Although computers are being used more and more, it can be useful to understand the difference between these types of records.

Running record

A running record is the short version. An easy way to remember this is a person runs to take a short cut. This is not to suggest that a worker should cut corners; rather what is needed is both a short and long version of events for recording purposes. Having a shorter version of a more detailed record available is extremely helpful when asked to write a chronology for a solicitor or for the court (see Chapter 5). It saves a worker time, because they do not have to plough back through a thick, heavy file or scroll down through numerous pages on the computer, which can literally take up a lot of work hours. Sometimes running records are known as *contact sheets*. They should show:

- at the top of the sheet: name of service user, date of birth, address. If the service user uses a different name from what is stated on their birth certificate or has a nickname, then this should be shown as well

- below the details of the service user: the date and time of event should be shown in a column and in another column a short written record (no more than two sentences). Sometimes it will be necessary to cross reference.

Example contact sheet

Background information

Sarah is a 23-year-woman with learning disabilities who is living in supported accommodation run by a voluntary organisation. Her key worker is Philippa Green, who has been worried recently about Sarah's mood changes and her reluctance to engage in her usual activities. These changes have occurred since Sarah started attending cookery classes at the local college. What follows is an extract from the contact sheet to which Philippa kept adding during the course of a week when her concerns about Sarah increased.

Extracts from contact sheet

SARAH PRIEST (DOB: 3.9.1987)

Likes to be called: Suzy

71 Herries Way, Churchtown C7 3TT

Monday 8 March 2010

13.10 Rang Mrs Brown, admin person at Niagra College, because Suzy had not returned from her cookery class; she is normally back by midday for lunch. Mrs Brown said she would ring back.

13.34 Mrs Brown rang back. Suzy has been in college. Course leader saw her walking out of the gates with several students after class.

14.02 Suzy came in. Really bad mood. Wanted her dinner. Would not say why she was late. After eating Suzy stayed in her room.

16.30 Went to say goodbye to Suzy in her bedroom. Obvious she had been crying. Said she was 'fine' and told me 'mind your own business.'

(signed) Philippa Green, Support Worker
8.3.10; 16.40

Monday 15 March 2010

12.30 Phone call from a Mrs Hathersage. She had found Suzy lying in an alleyway behind the shopping centre and crying. Suzy gave her the house number to ring but would not say where she lived. Agreed to go to pick up Suzy who was in Mrs Hathersage's house – 43 Walton Terrace (Tel: 123456).

12.55 Went with manager, Tom Walker, to pick up Suzy. Brought her back to the house.

13.15 Suzy refused food which is not like her and said she wanted to go to her room. She was not walking normally; I asked her why. She showed me injuries on her stomach and back which were still bleeding. Completed bodymap (placed in Section F on file). Suzy agreed to go to hospital.

13.30–19.20 At hospital with Suzy. Vanessa Eden, support worker, also came with us. Medical exam in casualty. Suzy told doctor she had been raped. Police contacted. See full write up in Section C on file.

21.20 Suzy asleep. Would not eat. Police to visit tomorrow – Lisa Grey, Vulnerable Adults Officer and someone else to discuss video interview.

21.25 Telephoned Tom (manager) to update him on the latest. I agreed I would come in tomorrow on my day off to support Suzy.

(signed) *Philippa Green, Support Worker*
15.3.10; 21.50

Process record

A process record is the long version of events. A common question from workers because managers can give conflicting advice is, 'How much should I write?' This is always difficult to answer because it depends on what you are writing and for whom you are writing it. The key word when contemplating writing a process record is *relevance*. A worker should never waffle on just to fill up the page or say, 'I put everything down to make sure I don't miss anything.' The objective of any process record is to:

- describe

- explain

- inform.

There are all sorts of reports which will be written for different purposes and target audiences. In order to make this relevant to safeguarding adults work, in this section we shall consider how to write a process record on a service user file when a worker has a particular concern, for example, an incident has been witnessed or the worker has received a disclosure. It is essential that a worker plans what they are going to record. In the busy world that everyone works in, workers often sit down when they can and immediately start to write without thinking about what they really need to say and without giving thought to how the information should be presented. Planning before writing is a good rule to adopt. People often do not want to be reminded of school and the lessons learnt there, but for any worker it is important to plan very much as you were taught to plan an essay or assignment; one needs to think about having a:

- beginning
- middle
- end.

In order to achieve this it is good to implement the following stages:

BEST PRACTICE POINTS
- Sit.
- Think.
- Plan.
- Draft.
- Read and check.
- Rewrite (and maybe rewrite again).

A worker should ask themselves the following three key questions whilst thinking and planning any record:

KEY QUESTIONS
- Why am I writing this record? (purpose)
- What do I need to say? (relevance)
- Who might read this? (access)

If any notes have been made at the time of the incident/disclosure the worker should re-read them at this planning stage. This will help the worker to reflect back accurately on what was said and done at the time.

Other key questions for the planning stage are:

KEY QUESTIONS

- Do I know this has definitely happened?
- How do I know this?
- Who saw this happen?
- Who did what and when?

During the planning stage a worker should reflect on some key subject areas which are pertinent to all written records before thinking about the actual content:

BEST PRACTICE POINTS

Before beginning to write, a worker should think about the following issues which will help them to focus, but some of these could also become subject areas within a record:
- fact
- opinion
- hearsay
- confidentiality
- consent to share information
- access to records.

Fact

In any written record it is vital to present the facts, that is what you know has definitely happened. This can relate to past or present circumstances or an event. A fact is information which can be used as evidence to prove that something has happened (finding of fact) and therefore facts need to be presented clearly and logically in a written report.

Opinion

Many workers are told they should not include their opinion in any records. This is bad advice. Opinion is a view or belief that may or may not be founded on proof or certainty. Any worker is entitled to express their opinion in a written record as long as they are qualified to do so.

For example, a court would not accept the opinion of a home care worker regarding the dating of injuries, but a doctor could give a professional opinion about this. However, the home care worker who has known a service user for five years may be able to express an opinion regarding a service user's ability to wash and dress themselves.

Expert's experience and comment

Opinions that suggest you have pre-conceived ideas or prejudices are not professional opinion. It is still best that whenever opinion is expressed in notes that all the other options are also noted. So if like me you sometimes use your notes as a kind of log to record your thinking, list the reasons and facts which support your views, but also list those that do not support them. At the end of it you can still provide a summary of what you think and why.

Steve Kirkpatrick

Hearsay

Hearsay means information which has been gained by someone but not directly witnessed by that person. A typical example might be: a social worker may be told by a neighbour as she arrives on the doorstep that the owner of the corner shop told her that he had heard Mrs X being shouted at by her husband last Saturday night outside his shop.

Confidentiality

A worker can always be challenged about whether they have kept confidentiality or, if it has been broken, whether this was justified. It is important for any worker to explain clearly to a service user what confidentiality means – emphasising that any information given to a worker belongs to the organisation they work for, not to the individual worker. In addition, there must be explanation regarding the circumstances when a worker must over-ride self-determination and break confidentiality. It is best practice for a worker to always record on a service user file when they have discussed confidentiality (on first contact with the service user or when the subject is revisited as the working relationship develops). Also when confidentiality has to be broken – maybe information shared – a worker must record the reasons for doing this and if appropriate under which statute they were acting.

Access to records

It has already been said earlier that a worker should always try to envisage who might have access to a record before starting to write a record. It is important to state whether a record has been shared with other people, or it is known that it will be shared in the future. For example, a bodymap should be completed whilst an injury is in front of the worker not from memory. A worker should record that the service user saw the completed map before the worker signed it.

In the planning stage a worker needs to think about content in the first instance, but then about how the information is going to be presented, namely, the layout. A record which is badly presented can irritate the reader who may be 'put off' reading it properly. So we need to look in more depth at content and layout within a process record.

Content

KEY WORDS FOR PLANNING CONTENT

- Purpose.
- Relevance.

We have all looked at records at some point and either thought, 'This is really good; it tells me a lot and it is well written,' or 'This is awful. I would never write like this.' So if a worker thinks back to these situations they need to ask themselves:

- What made the record good?
- What made the record bad?

This way of thinking will help a worker to participate in Exercises 4.1 and 4.2, which can be undertaken in a formal training course or in an individual's supervision session.

The content of any document should be:

- factual
- relevant
- objective

- clear
- concise
- accurate
- non-judgemental
- non-discriminatory.

EXERCISE 4.1

WHAT MAKES GOOD CONTENT?

OBJECTIVE
To make workers think about what makes a good written record.

PARTICIPANTS
Large group exercise or can be done in an individual supervision session.

EQUIPMENT
Trainer to use flipchart stand, paper and pens.

TIME
15 minutes.

TASK
1. Trainer asks the large group to think about what makes good content.
2. Trainer lists comments on flipchart paper.
3. Trainer facilitates open discussion.
4. Trainer pins sheets on wall after exercise is complete.

Geraldine Monaghan and her colleague Mark Pathak spend a lot of time writing reports for court. Geraldine explains their work and methodology, which supports what has been said above regarding the need to focus on purpose and relevance. Geraldine goes on to express her own views regarding good recording skills.

Expert's experience and comment

Mark writes a report then I go through it with him. There is a lot of stripping out. Key questions for us are: 'Why are we saying this?' and 'Does the Court need to know this?' There is a lot of testing – it is related to how the person will be as a witness. We may have a lot of social history but it may not need to go in. Both sets of Counsel and the Judge will see this. Anything that has a bearing on how the person will be as witness will be in.

Electronic records frame the work flow, but shouldn't dictate it. There can be a view that electronic systems define the order, shape and content of records without adequately capturing professional practice. Electronic records don't simply require data inputting; they provide the framework we use for analysis. So what if there were three phone calls? What did it all mean? Analyse what was said. It is essential to capture and record professional assessment and case management decisions. Key words are ANALYSIS and REFLECTION. As a manager, if a worker goes off sick, the record should tell you who the service user is, why we're involved, what the worker is doing and why.

Geraldine Monaghan

Layout

How a written record looks will affect the reader; if one sees hard to read or untidy handwriting it is immediately off-putting. Good layout is an important part of recording. A worker needs to think about how they will present written information and in order to do this planning once again plays an important role. In training or a supervision session, it is helpful to go through the different ways in which a record can be set out. This should be done in an interesting way, not in a school like fashion, which may bring back bad memories for some people. Exercise 4.2 will be one way of facilitating this.

It is important that a worker realises that different things can be used to make the presentation attractive to the reader namely:

- legible handwriting

- black pen

- paragraphs

- headings/sub-headings

- numbering/lettering, for example, 1, 2, 3; (i) (ii) (iii); (a), (b), (c)

- bullet points

- asterisks

- capitals

- bold

- italics

- underline

- quotations

- punctuation, spelling and grammar.

EXERCISE 4.2
WHAT MAKES GOOD LAYOUT?

OBJECTIVE
To make workers think how to present a written record.

PARTICIPANTS
Large group exercise.

EQUIPMENT
Trainer to use flipchart stand, paper and pens.

TIME
15 minutes.

TASK
1. Trainer asks the large group to think about what makes a written record look good.
2. Trainer lists comments on flipchart paper.
3. Trainer facilitates open discussion.
4. Trainer pins sheets on wall after exercise is complete.

It is important that text is set out in such a way that it is easy to find information if the reader needs to refer back to something. There is nothing more off-putting than seeing pages and pages of writing with no breaks in it. Therefore the use of paragraphs, headings, sub-headings and numbering can be helpful to the reader, but the writer must be consistent in what they choose to do. The use of headings and sub-headings are good examples.

Examples of good and bad recording

Bad use of heading and sub-headings:

Categories of abuse alleged

<u>PHYSICAL ABUSE</u>

Text written by worker about this type of abuse

Financial Abuse

Text written by worker about this type of abuse

Good use of heading and sub-headings:

CATEGORIES OF ABUSE ALLEGED:

(i)   Physical abuse

   Text written by worker about this type of abuse

(ii)   Financial abuse

   Text written by worker about this type of abuse

Learning point:

The bad example above illustrates the lack of punctuation and it is not clear how headings are being used. There is inconsistency in the use of capitals, bold and underlining for the headings regarding the categories of abuse. The second category does not stand out at all; the writer had made the first category stand out more so by using bold and underlining the words.

Using quotations

It is very good and helpful in safeguarding adults work if a worker can actually quote exactly what a victim, abuser or witness said, but the worker needs to be able to evidence that these were the exact words which were spoken at the time. This is where the importance of note-taking and keeping contemporaneous notes comes into play. When receiving a disclosure unexpectedly a worker can be ill-prepared and may have to rely on memory to a certain degree; therefore quotes within a process record or report should not be lengthy unless a worker has the original notes, otherwise the validity will be questioned. If during a formal investigation interview one of the interviewers has been taking notes more or less verbatim, then it would be alright to quote at length if this was felt to be needed.

It is important to note that some computer software packages will not allow swear words to be written. Workers need to contact their IT people if this happens. If it needs to be recorded that a service user has been verbally abusive it is important to quote the exact words used.

Punctuation, spelling and grammar

It is important that a worker uses punctuation, spelling and grammar correctly. If a worker feels they are weak in any of these areas they need to read some of the texts which are suggested at the end of this chapter. If it comes to light that a worker has some literacy problems, a manager should ensure that they receive some proper help. If there are mistakes in any record, then it shows the worker up in a bad light and they might not be taken seriously. It looks shoddy if there are mistakes in any record and can give the impression that the worker has not taken time or care with their recording. It is always important to check what you have written.

Another common question on training courses is whether the first or third person should be used. Some organisations' recording policies give clear guidance on this, depending on the type of written record. In general there is nothing wrong with using either the first person or the third person; workers just need to be consistent in what they choose to do.

Avoid using abbreviations and acronyms

We all take short cuts to make life easier. When we take notes we all write in our own special shorthand; we know what we mean! However, when recording properly on a service user file or writing a report, abbreviations and acronyms must be avoided. Ideally when one needs to shorten to an abbreviation the correct way is to write the full version and put the acronym in brackets, which can then be used in the text that follows, for example:

> I rang DS Ian Slater in the Public Protection Unit (PPU) to invite him to the strategy meeting. He said that it was unlikely that anyone from the PPU could attend on that day because his two colleagues were currently off sick.

We all use our own form of jargon when we speak and it becomes part of the language we use at work. We should be mindful that phrases or terms come in and out fashion too: 'it has been taken on board'; 'I hear what you're saying'; 'I'll flag that up'; 'It's a safeguarding issue'; 'Let's move on'. However, to someone not working in the same field or to a service user it could seem that a foreign language is being spoken. This must be borne in mind when writing on records too, that is, when using abbreviations or referring to places that other people don't know what they are.

Examples of bad recording

- Mrs Bowman was taken to PGI when she was found unconscious.

- Bill had regularly attended Somerset Road for the past two years. It was only in the last six months that staff started to notice changes in him.

- The VA1 had been faxed through.

- Did the interview during the morning in Sefton.

It is always hard to stop workers using abbreviations completely. If a particular team or group of workers regularly use the same abbreviations it is acceptable to develop a glossary and put the glossary on the front of a service user's paper file.

EXERCISE 4.3
ABBREVIATIONS

OBJECTIVE

To make workers realise how many abbreviations they use in their written records.

PARTICIPANTS

Small groups.

EQUIPMENT

Flipchart paper and pens.

TIME

10 minutes.

TASK

1. Participants are asked to think about the abbreviations they use when they write any document for recording purposes. This will include the shortening of names and titles of institutions, etc.

2. Each group will list the abbreviations on the flipchart sheet.

FEEDBACK

The trainer will ask a person in each group to read down the list (without translating/explaining the term) but pausing after each abbreviation. Others are asked to be honest and shout out if they do not know the meaning of something. Participants are also asked to shout out if the abbreviations could have two meanings (e.g. HV = home visit or health visitor; NFA = no further action or no fixed abode).

What follows is a random collection of abbreviations which have been taken from various training courses when this exercise has been undertaken. The reader might like to do a quick exercise to see:

- how many abbreviations for which they believe they know the meanings

- how many for which they have no idea about the meaning

- those which could have two meanings.

ABC	DPs	PH
ACC	DV	POVA
AD	DWP	PP
ADV	FSU	PPU
ADL	GP	PRN
AL	HA	PSD
AS	HB	PSW
ASC	HV	RA
BATT locality	ILF	Randall
CAMHS	IMCA	SAP
CAT	Instit2	SHO
CC	IS	SM
CMHT	MAPPA	SNR PRAC
COPD	MAR	SNT
COSHH	MARAC	SOB
CPN	MCA	SOVA
CQC	MHN	SPD
CRB	MHT	SS/SSD
CSU	MS	St George's
CSW	NFA	START
CVA	NHS	SU
CW	NOK	SVA
DASCAS	OA	SW
DC	OT	TC
DH	OV	ZF
DIS	P.ASS	TM
DN	PC	TQR
DOB	PCT	TOIL
Dom care	PD	VA

The following experience from Steve Kirkpatrick shows how using abbreviations can lead someone to make an assumption about the writer:

Expert's experience and comment

But definitely try not to use any abbreviations that might be misconstrued. In 1988 in my notes I abbreviated descriptions of Pakistani to 'paki' for speed of note-taking. The barrister during a subsequent Crown Court case remarked to one of my colleagues that he thought I was racist. I didn't think I was, but it made me look unprofessional.

Steve Kirkpatrick

Note-taking

Note-taking will be mentioned frequently during Chapters 6 and 7, but it is important to say in this chapter that note-taking is important in day-to-day work. A worker should always carry a notebook with them – no matter how small – so that if something does need to be recorded the worker can access paper quickly and it can be kept safe. It does not look very professional if a worker scribbles on the back of a cigarette packet or on the inside of their cheque book. We shall see later just how important notes can become as evidence but in day-to-day work they can act as an aide-memoire and help a worker in planning to write up on a service user file or in producing some sort of report.

BEST PRACTICE POINTS
- State time and date when notes started to be taken.
- Try to make notes meaningful, so that they will trigger the memory.
- Notes should be legible to the note-taker.
- Actual quotes should be clearly marked.
- State time and date notes completed.
- Sign the notes.

Expert's experience and comment

We all have occasions when we do not keep good enough records. I know I am still guilty of this. I think we are sometimes just too busy and it takes a great deal of tenacity to keep it up. I *think if we can get in the habit of taking notes on everything we do then we will automatically have the right records when we need them. But I know that with data protection issues it is not always easy to do what I do. I have a desk job and a laptop always on, so it is far easier for me to keep more copious notes. Also if professionals make diary notes of what they do as if they will be scrutinised, then habits are formed which show the steps we take with all our observations and decisions. Our impartiality tends to come across better.*

Steve Kirkpatrick

Reviewing

Workers will be familiar with the term 'review' in terms of reviewing medication, health, care packages, care plans, risk assessments, safeguarding plans and so on. In other words there might be lots of different things that need to be reviewed. Organisations may have a particular form which needs to be completed before and after a review takes place. When reviews are undertaken then it is important that they are prepared for before the event takes place and recorded properly when decisions have been made about the future. It is important to say within this chapter that written records themselves should be reviewed regularly, not just in line with other types of reviews.

Where process records are kept on long-term cases then best practice is to review every three months. We shall be looking at reviewing safeguarding adults work later in the book, but for now it is important to summarise that in a review of any process recording, a worker should be reflecting on:

- objectives
- achievements/failures
- problems/difficulties
- developments
- reassessment of risk
- other assessments needed
- summary
- conclusion
- recommendations.

Managers' responsibilities

Managers should regularly read their workers' case files in order to know how they are recording. Many managers groan when this is said because they say they have not got time to do this; this is very dangerous practice. Recording is of paramount importance and a manager needs to check that a worker is recording properly. Assumptions should never be made. A manager should ideally be supervising from case files. Before a planned supervision session a manager should read several files; a supervision policy usually states what the minimum should be. During the supervision session the files – whether paper or electronic – should be available. Any major decisions regarding a case made within the session should be recorded in the supervision notes but also within the file. Any disagreements between manager and worker should also be recorded.

EXERCISE 4.4
WHAT DID YOU DO THIS MORNING?

OBJECTIVE
To see how a worker currently records.

PARTICIPANTS
Individual.

EQUIPMENT
Paper and pen.

TIME
10 minutes.

TASK

1. The worker is given a blank A4 sheet of paper and asked to imagine that it is either the computer screen on which they normally write records, or the recording sheet they use to record if they keep paper files.
2. The worker is asked to write a true written record of what she or he has done from the time they woke up on that day until they walked into work that day.

FEEDBACK
The manager will read the record and give constructive feedback.

A manager has the right to check files at anytime. Workers should not see this as 'checking up' but rather a positive step to ensuring accountability. A manager should write on a file when it has been accessed. The following exercises are included so that managers in any setting can use them in supervision to ascertain how a worker records. This can be really useful when a new worker has been appointed.

EXERCISE 4.5

RECORDING WHAT YOU SEE

OBJECTIVE
To practice observational skills and recording skills.

PARTICIPANTS
Stage 1 will be undertaken individually; participants will then work in pairs and larger groups.

EQUIPMENT
Trainer to provide a DVD which shows several short scenes in quick succession.[1]
Paper and pens.

TIME
30 minutes.

TASK

1. Trainer shows part of a DVD.

2. Participants are asked to write a true written record of what they have just watched.

3. Participants go into pairs and give their partner the written record to read. They then discuss what was good, bad, etc. about the record and crucially whether it was accurate.

FEEDBACK
Group discussion to focus on accuracy, content, layout, etc.

---

1   Case scenarios can be found on the DVDs in the 'Working with Adult Abuse Series' produced by Jacki Pritchard Ltd. See www.jackipritchard.co.uk.

EXERCISE 4.6

RECORDING WHAT YOU HEAR

OBJECTIVE
To practise listening, observational and recording skills.

PARTICIPANTS
Stage 1 will be undertaken individually; participants will then work in pairs and larger groups.

EQUIPMENT
Paper and pens.

TIME
30 minutes.

TASK

1.   A dialogue will take place for 5 minutes between two participants in front of the rest of the group. The trainer will give the pair a subject to talk about.

2.   Participants are asked to write a true written record of what they have just watched.

3.   Participants go into pairs and give their partner the written record to read. They then discuss what was good, bad, etc. about the record.

FEEDBACK
Group discussion to focus on accuracy, content, layout, etc.

Involving service users' in recording

Whenever writing about a service user it is vital to include that person's views. Workers in many different jobs often fail to think about asking a service user to contribute to their own record; rarely are files shown or shared with a service user on a regular basis. A worker should remember that such involvement is promoting working in partnership with the service user. It is imperative that a service user's views, opinions and feelings are recorded. This will be explored more fully in Chapter 6.

Conclusion

We would like to end this chapter by giving the reader a simple list of DOs and DON'Ts for their day-to-day practice followed by some advice from a very experienced police officer. The advice given relates to general recording which can become evidence later in abuse cases and prepares the reader for the chapters on evidential requirements.

BEST PRACTICE POINTS: DOS AND DON'TS FOR RECORDING

DO:
- state the time and date of all visits, incidents, conversations, actions
- always put your signature, job title, time and date at the end of a note/record
- use black pen
- cross out mistakes with just one black line and initial
- check what you have written
- use a dictionary or spell check (make sure the correct language is set on the computer)
- use a thesaurus if you become aware that you use the same words too often
- record regularly
- record as soon as possible after an event.

DON'T:
- use a pencil
- use Tippex
- write long sentences
- be vague
- waffle
- use jargon
- use clichés
- use shorthand
- use abbreviations.

Expert's experience and comment

Recordings should be as contemporaneous as possible; drafted in detailed, fair, factual, balanced, coherent, and idiomatic language. Where necessary they should explain the process and rationale of risk assessment and elaborate and justify any action taken. Opinion should be made distinct from the recording of facts.

They should be owned by their author or authors – a professional, honest and transparent evidential account written in a mindset that expects them to be understood by an investigator, examined and maybe challenged in court.

My experience tells me that the crime is often in the detail and provenance of recording. The recording benchmark should be set at 'excellent' and the learning of the processes and skills to meet this standard should be at the heart of professional training and development. Any recording in the context of working with a vulnerable adult should be made in the expectation of there being a safeguarding issue at some time and in some place. In contrast to the value of exemplary recording, poorly kept (and protected) records or recordings that amount to no more than furtive 'secret diaries' can hamper fair investigations, negate justice and result in missed opportunities to safeguard.

Police Officer

Suggested reading

Cutts, M. (2009) *Oxford Guide to Plain English.* 3rd edition. Oxford: Oxford University Press.

Hilton, C. and Hyder, M. (1992) *Getting to Grips with Punctuation and Grammar.* London: Letts Educational.

Seely, J. (2009) *Oxford A–Z of Punctuation and Grammar.* 2nd edition. Oxford: Oxford University Press.

Chapter 5

Tools for Effective Recording

Recording need not be boring; it can actually become exciting if a worker endeavours to be creative by using different tools. Unfortunately because the demand for paperwork (mainly forms) to be completed has grown so much in the last decade or so, there can be a lack of incentive to record in an original way. Also workers need to have been introduced to different ways of recording in order to do it. A lot can be learnt from tools which have been used in child protection work and which are also appropriate for work with adults. Bodymaps are one such tool, but genograms and ecomaps are also very useful. Such tools are the subject of this chapter.

Bodymaps

Doctors and nurses will be familiar with bodymaps, but other workers may be reluctant to use them because they might be under the misapprehension that they should have a medical background to undertake this task. This is not the case at all. A bodymap is a simple tool for recording any injuries which might be seen by a worker on a service user's body, that is, it is an observational tool. Examples of bodymaps are given on the following pages in Figures 5.1, 5.2 and 5.3.

It is important to emphasise that a worker should *never* ask a service user to take off their clothes in order to see an injury (unless they are a medical professional and have just cause); a worker only records what they see naturally. For example, a care worker may see a service user with a black eye and a cut lip when they arrive at the day centre; another worker in a care home may see bruising on a resident's back when they are helping them to bath or to dress.

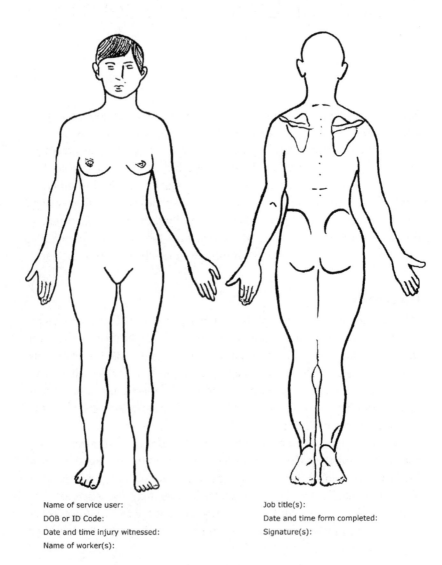

Name of service user: Job title(s):

DOB or ID Code: Date and time form completed:

Date and time injury witnessed: Signature(s):

Name of worker(s):

Figure 5.1 Female bodymap: front and back views

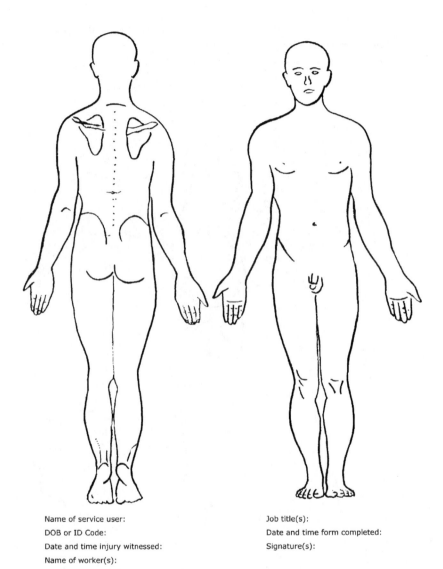

Name of service user: Job title(s):
DOB or ID Code: Date and time form completed:
Date and time injury witnessed: Signature(s):
Name of worker(s):

Figure 5.2 Male bodymap: back and front views

Name of service user: Job title(s):

DOB or ID Code: Date and time form completed:

Date and time injury witnessed: Signature(s):

Name of worker(s):

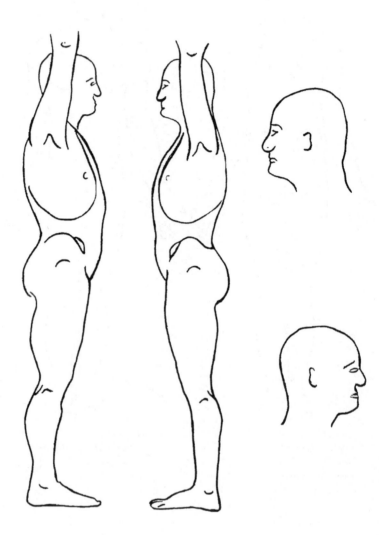

Figure 5.3 Bodymap: side views

A worker should draw what they see; and no-one is expected to be a brilliant artist. It is just a matter of drawing an outline on a bodymap. For example, a line will be used to draw a scratch or cut. If a bruise is visible the shape of the bruise should be drawn. A line can be drawn from the injury to a space on the bodymap where a short description can be written, for example:

- cut, approximately 5 cm long

- bruise, round in shape – approximately 2 cm in diameter; yellow colour.

A worker should never speculate how the injury has occurred. If a worker actually witnessed a service user self-harm by cutting themselves with a razor blade, the cuts would be drawn on a bodymap, but an incident form would also need to be completed and a separate record would be written up on the service user file explaining what had happened.

Organisations may be using bodymaps but without any details, for example those regarding the service user, worker, date and time when the form was completed or guidance for staff about how to use bodymaps correctly.

Example of bad practice

Shauna Hathaway, manager of a care home, encouraged her staff to complete bodymaps whenever a resident incurred an injury and they regularly did this. Bodymaps were kept within the residents' case files, which were stored in a filing cabinet in the main office. Gail, the administrator, decided that the filing cabinet needed sorting out and decided to put an afternoon aside to do this. Just as she had a lot of files in her arms a care worker came into the room and the door hit Gail; the files went up in the air and then dropped on the floor. Papers, including bodymaps, were scattered all over the floor. None of the bodymaps had names on or signatures of staff who had completed them. There was no way of knowing which bodymap belonged in which file.

BEST PRACTICE POINTS

On a bodymap you must write:
- name of service user
- date of birth
- date and time the injury was first witnessed
- date and time the bodymap was completed
- name of worker(s) completing the bodymap
- job title(s)
- signature(s).

All of the above are essential because it is vital that the bodymap can be linked directly to a particular person, but also that exact times are recorded. Ideally workers should always carry bodymaps with them but in reality they can be sitting on the back seat of a car or located in a filing cabinet in an office. If a worker has to go to get a bodymap after seeing an injury, it is important to record when they first saw the injury and how much later they completed the bodymap. A bodymap should never be completed from memory; it should be drawn when the injuries are directly in view of the worker. Hence the need to be very upfront and honest with a service user from the first contact about what records are kept within an organisation. A service user needs to be made aware that if a worker sees an injury it is part of their job to record what they have seen. If this has been explained well at the beginning of a working relationship, then it should not come as a shock when a worker says they need to complete a bodymap.

An original bodymap should never be altered or added to in any way. It has been known for workers to add injuries onto one bodymap and date the addition. One of the main objectives of keeping bodymaps on file is that it becomes clearly visible to a worker just how many bodymaps are being completed in certain cases. If bodymaps are being completed on a regular basis then this should cause the worker to question what is occurring in this situation. This is why a bodymap is referred to as a monitoring tool.

Example of bad practice

Workers in Mountjoy Care Home had been asked by their manager, Julie, to keep bodymaps on Ethel Raynor (who came in for regular respite stays) because it was suspected that she was a victim of domestic violence. There were problems within the care home regarding communication and some staff openly resented having to keep records. Julie came in one morning and saw in the communication book that the one of the night staff, Ros, had written she was worried about Ethel. It was recorded that Ethel had been admitted last night and had bruising on her right shoulder. Julie went to look at Ethel's file and found two bodymaps; one had been completed by Ros at 22.00. the previous night. The form had been completed with good detail and the bruise was drawn on the right shoulder blade, being described as 'blue/purple in colour; the size of a 50p piece'. The other bodymap had been completed by Tracey, a care worker; she had put the date and her own name on the bodymap but did not put Ethel's name or the time she had seen the bruise. The thing that really worried Julie was that a circle had been drawn in the middle of the back and the word 'bruise' written next to it. Julie was looking at two bodymaps which were supposed to be true observations of the same bruise, but in fact were drawn on completely different parts of the body.

Learning points:
- If a bodymap has been completed by one member of staff already then there is no need for other staff to record it again unless additional injuries occur and a fresh bodymap should be completed.

- Staff should always read a communication book when coming on duty. If Tracey had done this she would have known that Ros had already completed a bodymap.

- Bodymaps must be accurate.

- All details need to be completed on a bodymap.

Example of good practice

Jo was a support worker who was supporting Danny, an adult with moderate learning disabilities, to live independently in a flat. Jo had had concerns that Danny was being financially abused by two young men who he had met in the local pub. She had made a safeguarding alert but nothing had come of it because Danny said the men were his friends. Jo's concerns arose again when Danny started getting a lot of black eyes and bruising on his face. Her manager told her to complete bodymaps as and when she saw any injuries. Jo was very open with Danny about her concerns and why she was completing the bodymaps. On Monday 25 January when Jo called for Danny at 10.00 a.m. to go shopping with him, she saw that he had a cut lip and his right cheek was very red. Danny said he had walked into the bathroom door. Jo completed a bodymap. Danny always looked forward to going food shopping on a Monday morning, but on this day he was very agitated and said he must be back home by 11.00 a.m. but would not say why. He was also reluctant to spend any money. Jo just felt there was something wrong, so later in the day she decided to call in again to see Danny just to check that he was OK. When she arrived at 16.30 Danny had two more cuts on his face and a black eye. He was adamant he had walked into the same door again. Jo completed a new bodymap.

Sometimes professionals have certain practices that may hinder the progression of evidence to court. A good example is that of nurses who record when an injury/wound has healed. Some nurses put a line through an injury they have drawn previously when it is healed and add the date next to the line when they have done this. It would be better to draw the injury again on a new bodymap and draw the line there. Changing the original bodymaps could be seen as tampering with evidence.

Bodymaps can be used as a monitoring tool in all sorts of situations, but they are being discussed here because they can be used as evidence to prove that abuse has happened. It is stated several times in this book that it can take years to prove that abuse has occurred. If a case eventually gets to court, bodymaps which were completed years ago can be used as evidence if it is thought they can add weight to the case.

Other types of monitoring protocols

Professionals monitor situations for different reasons, that is, they will have their own objectives in doing this and will use appropriate tools to measure whatever they are monitoring. We know that abuse often remains well hidden and therefore it is hard to identify it. A way to prove whether abuse has happened or not can be to monitor changes in behaviour, lifestyle, attitude, mood and so on. Workers who have long-term working relationships with people can have a major role in identifying abuse because they should be able to pick up on changes as they occur. A worker should always record any change they notice no matter how small. Monitoring tools can be developed to record such changes. It is useful to look back at some very simple tools which were developed in North America years ago by nursing professionals who were researching elder abuse. They developed tools for the alleged older victim and the carer who was the alleged abuser (Fulmer 1984; Ross *et al.* 1985). These tools have been adapted and used in the UK since the 1990s (see Davies 1993 and 1997)

Photographs

Just whilst we are talking about observing and recording injuries, some mention should be made of photographs. Photographs of injuries can make good evidence, but they have to be taken in the correct way. This means they should be taken either by a Police Forensic Surgeon or within a hospital setting. This is because we are living in an age when technology is highly developed and moving forward all the time. Therefore, if someone is very good with technology they could alter the image of a photograph taken on a mobile telephone or digital camera. For example a bruise could be made bigger or changed to a different colour. In any case, workers should be mindful of the fact that they should not take photographs without the consent of a person; it is an intrusion on their privacy and human rights.

Examples of bad practice

Example 1

A newly qualified social worker had been asked by her manager to go and get some more information from an alleged victim after an alert came in. This worker had not read the safeguarding adults policy and had not been on any training regarding adult abuse; so she did as she was asked not realising that by going to speak to the alleged victim she could be contaminating evidence or actually starting an investigation before a strategy meeting had taken place. When she visited the alleged victim in her own home, she saw that the woman had a lot of injuries on her face, arms and legs. The woman admitted that her brother had been violent towards her but she did not want to take it further. The social worker said, 'I respect your self-determination, but I just need to take some evidence back for my line manager' and immediately got her mobile phone out and started to take photographs of the woman.

Example 2

Two agency staff, Carol and Jenny, who were working temporarily in a care home were worried about the practices of the workers who had worked in the home for many years. They talked to each other about the fact they thought some residents were grossly neglected; many stayed in bed for most of the day; certain staff shouted and swore at residents on a regular basis. They felt they could not go to the manager of the home, who had worked there for 22 years, because she was very open about the friendships she had outside the workplace with these particular members of staff. Carol and Jenny decided to take matters into their own hands. They secretly took photographs of residents who they felt were malnourished and had pressure sores; they also carried dictaphones in their pockets so they could record conversations they heard.

Illustrating relationships

Social history can be a very important part of the work we undertake with an abused person, whether it be a child or an adult. It is important to understand what has happened to a person in the past in order to comprehend why they might be as they are now. It is very necessary to have an understanding of why a person is acting in a certain way and presenting particular behaviours rather than just sticking a label on them, for example, 'attention seeking', 'has challenging behaviour'. Very often the root cause of a current abusive situation stems back to something which happened many years ago – a particular loss, incident, relationship, feud, etc. So it can be key to get a clear picture of past and current relationships.

Writing the social history in words can be informative, but where there are many or complex relationships it is sometimes helpful to see them visually. Many child abuse inquiries and serious case reviews have highlighted the fact that often agencies and organisations have masses of information about families within case records, and trawling through them to summarise key information can be extremely difficult as well as very time consuming.

So this is where both genograms and ecomaps can be very useful; but what are they? Before answering the question it is important to say that both tools can be used as a way of presenting information when working with a case of abuse, namely, presenting information through the visual format within case files, reports for case conferences or court. In addition these tools can be used in therapeutic sessions which will be discussed further below.

Genograms

The easy way to remember what a genogram portrays is to link the word to genealogy – family tree and family history. We are going to keep this simple because the use of genograms has been developed greatly in the past 25 years and the methodology used can be complex. By that we mean that too many things are portrayed on the genogram for future analysis. This is because this method of working is now adopted by many different professionals and therapists in their day-to-day practice. This is demonstrated in this definition of a genogram:

DEFINITION OF GENOGRAM

A person's family relationships and medical history displayed visually. Unlike a traditional family tree, the user is able to picture hereditary and psychological factors that define relationships. A genogram is useful for identifying repetitive behaviour patterns and to recognise hereditary trends.

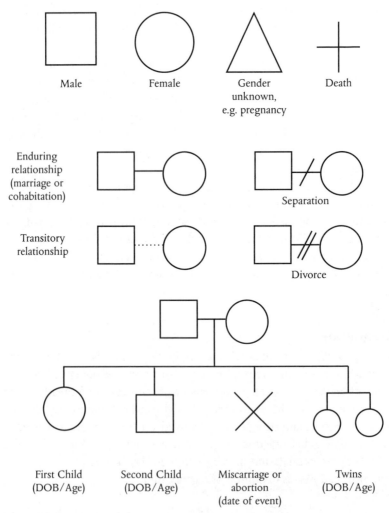

Figure 5.6 Genogram symbols

Our intention is to give the reader simple tools to use, not to make life more difficult. For many years in work with children, life story work has been undertaken; with older adults reminiscence work is used. A genogram can simply be the drawing of a family tree, and it can be a rewarding piece of work to do with an adult if they are willing to get involved in drawing the genogram themselves. If for some reason the adult could not actively engage in drawing themselves, then with their agreement a worker could draw the genogram whilst engaging in conversation with the adult.

When the term 'family tree' is used the reader may visualise a tree with branches as symbolised by the BBC programme 'Who Do You Think You Are?' A genogram involves the use of symbols rather than a traditional tree; this method was first developed by McGoldrick and Gerson (1985) but nowadays there is a wealth of books and software packages which have been developed for different professionals. Some very basic symbols are shown in Figure 5.6, but it is suggested the reader should explore further and gain more knowledge regarding the symbols they have use for in their work.

Some people love using symbols; others struggle to utilise them. For the purposes of safeguarding adults work it will suffice to have knowledge of the basic symbols and to keep the genograms simple. Pritchard has developed exercises for training sessions so that workers can draw genograms for past and current cases (see Exercise 5.1). What is usually highlighted is that there is knowledge about the current family situation, but rarely has work been undertaken about the past. Pritchard's experiences evidence the fact that many workers are not regularly getting information about past generations and relationships in order to write good social histories. When asked about this, a common response from course participants is, 'We haven't got time to do this.' This is not a good enough excuse. We need to undertake good social histories to understand a person and their history; using creative tools will help to do this in an effective and rewarding way both for the service user and the worker.

If a worker is going to produce a genogram for a case file or to put in a report, then the traditional symbols should be used. However, if a service user wants to draw a traditional tree with branches, then that should be encouraged as it is yet another way of promoting the service user to contribute their own record.

Ecomap

We see the genogram as a starting point and forming the basis for developing an ecomap. It seems some professionals and therapists try to amalgamate the two. An ecomap can be defined as:

DEFINITION OF ECOMAP

A graphical representation of the systems that feature in a person's life.

Like the genogram it is good to get the adult involved in drawing this map because it is about illustrating how the adult sees their relationships with people and organisations. The worker may view things differently and if this is the case then separate maps should be drawn and used to facilitate discussions about why the worker and service user have different views. Ecomaps were first developed by Ann Hartman in the 1970s, and the reader is encouraged to read more about how ecomaps can be developed (Hartman 1995). We think it is important to let the service user decide how they want to draw the ecomap. There should be no hard and fast rules; just the starting point that the service user should be at the centre of the map.

Both people and organisations should be depicted; this can be done in a circle, triangle, square – it does not matter. Then the idea is to show how the person views that relationship, for example:

STRONG
WEAK
STRESSFUL

Victim's ecomap: case example of Debra

The following ecomap was drawn by Debra, a 46-year-old woman who has been a victim of child sexual abuse and domestic violence. Debra is known to a local community mental health team and had several compulsory admissions to hospital several years ago. She used to regularly attempt suicide, but during the past four years she has been working through the healing process and is now well on the way to recovery.

In recent months Debra has drawn several versions of an ecomap because professionals were going in and out of her life. She agreed to this version of her ecomap being printed in the book (see Figure 5.7).

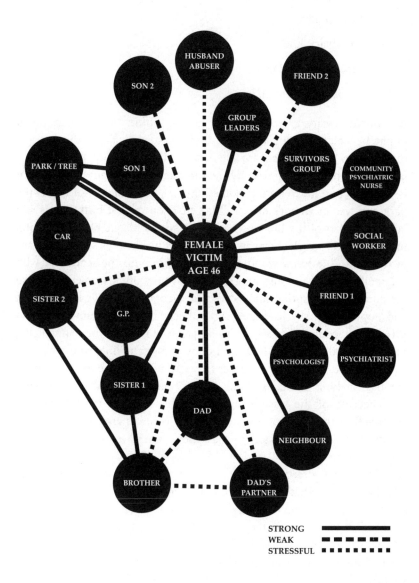

Figure 5.7 Example of ecomap

In another version Debra used colours to depict her emotions and created the following grid:

- good (orange line)
- love (yellow line)
- bad (black line)
- dislike (green line)
- awkward (red line).

It is not necessary to explain every person within Debra's map, but it might be helpful to the reader to understand why Debra drew some things on it. It is important for the person who is drawing an ecomap to understand that they can put anything in there if they want to do so, that is, if it is important to portray something. A good example of this is the park and tree in Debra's map. Debra's first son died at birth. He is still very much part of her life. She had a tree with a plaque planted for him in a local park, which she visits very frequently. She says she finds peace in the park. She has a wonderful relationship with the gardeners who originally planted the tree, and has got to know other women who also get comfort from sitting under the tree. Debra has always felt 'trapped and imprisoned'; she loves her car and sees it as important because it gives her freedom and gets her to a place she needs to be, namely, the park. This is the reason why Debra drew two strong lines to the park.

There are also two lines to her father to illustrate the mixed feelings she has for him. She talks about 'loving him' but also about 'disliking him' because of the way he has abused her and her mother (who is deceased) in the past but also the way he controls and treats her now. In other ecomaps she has drawn a yellow line [love] and a green line [dislike] to her father.

Debra is divorced from the husband who abused her; her second son lives with his father. They are both drawn on the map because they only live a couple of miles away and Debra often bumps into them. The husband does not allow the son to speak to Debra. Extreme physical and sexual violence was inflicted on Debra by her husband, usually in the bathroom. There were occasions when she was nearly drowned. She cannot take a bath or shower because of these experiences (she sponge washes herself) and experiences what she calls 'night terrors'. Therefore, her husband is still very much in her life and hence is on the map.

EXERCISE 5.1

DRAWING A GENOGRAM AND AN ECOMAP

OBJECTIVE
To have the opportunity to develop both a genogram and an ecomap for one case.

PARTICIPANTS
Ideally this exercise should be undertaken in small groups, for example, four people.

EQUIPMENT
Flipchart paper and lots of different coloured flipchart pens.

TIME
30 minutes to work in groups.
15 minutes allocated for each group to feedback their work and for discussion.

TASK
1. Before participants are split into smaller groups the trainer needs to identify participants who could talk about a case of abuse – either from the past or the present. One such person will be put in each group.

2. The person talks about their case. As s/he is doing this other members of the group will start drawing both the genogram and the ecomap. This should be done whilst full discussion takes place between the group members and there should be agreement about how the information is presented on both the genogram and ecomap.

FEEDBACK
1. One group at a time will display and talk through their genogram and ecomap.

2. When the drawings are pinned up but before feedback is given, the trainer should ask other groups to express their initial reactions to what they see in front of them.

3. It is preferable for a group member other than the person whose case it is to talk through the genogram and ecomap. People should be encouraged *not* to tell the abuse story as it has been disclosed in the group, but rather to give a 'guided tour' through the two drawings.

4. Questions and discussion then follows.

When this method of therapy was first introduced to Debra she was amazed when she finished drawing to see just how many people she had in the map and how many strong lines. She often feels 'lonely and isolated,' so this was a positive experience for her but also gave a direction and purpose to future work. This illustrates perfectly how both genograms and ecomaps can be used therapeutically.

Workers can draw genograms or ecomaps during training sessions using past or current cases, but obviously having to draw them from the perspective of how they think the service user views their relationships. It is always interesting to see people's facial expressions when the ecomap is put up on the flipchart stand or wall and to ask people what they see immediately.

How genograms and ecomaps can be used in safeguarding meetings

It has already been said above that drawing genograms and ecomaps can be helpful when doing direct work with a service user because it gives insight into a person's past, but also how they view things now. To summarise, they can be both assessment and therapeutic tools, but how do they fit into safeguarding adults work? We would advocate that if these tools were used in day-to-day work, they would already be available if and when a strategy meeting had to be convened. However, it is very unlikely to be the case until it becomes common practice in this area of work. These tools could be developed during the course of an investigation and be included in the investigating officer's report to a case conference. The drawings would be scaled down and scanned. The original could also be displayed at the case conference. This has been known to happen and it has been really helpful to participants at the case conference; one person said, 'Seeing the ecomap gave me more understanding than reading names of people I have never met in a report.' This way of working could also be written in a safeguarding plan when planning the long-term work with either a victim or an abuser who is also a vulnerable adult.

Chronologies

We now need to turn to the use of chronologies. We think a chronology should be maintained as routine and a running document in every safeguarding case and possibly every case of any type. There are simply too many examples of busy workers looking exclusively or primarily at the presenting incident. A file chronology is a crucial way of enabling people to see the new incident in context. A useful phrase to remember is, 'warnings should be seen as cumulative'; chronologies are a vital way of enabling people to do this.

Solicitors both in a local authority and the Crown Prosecution Service will usually ask a worker for a chronology; they like to have a summary of events and therefore this can be a crucial part of the recording process in safeguarding adults work. However, chronologies are not developed solely for legal purposes; different professionals may use them to summarise their work with someone. In child protection they are used for the core assessment process. By definition a chronology is 'the arrangement of events or dates in the order of their occurrence' (Oxford English Dictionary). Therefore, they are useful because at a quick glance a worker can see what happened and when.

With heavy caseloads and a lot of throughput workers cannot be expected to remember the exact timing of everything that has happened whilst working on a case. Also in some settings the turnover of staff is high, so it is important that a worker taking over a case (or coming to work in a communal setting) can see at a glance the relevant history of a service user and the sequence of events. Chronologies can be used in conjunction with contact sheets (see Chapter 4) which will help to expand on the information. Contact sheets can be attached to the back of a chronology which has been written. Summaries which are discussed below also help in the construction of chronologies.

If a worker has never written a chronology for legal purposes, then it is wise to seek advice in the first instance from the solicitor who is requesting the chronology. Below are some headings which might be useful for a basic chronology.

SUBJECT HEADINGS FOR A CHRONOLOGY

A chronology should include detail about (if applicable):

- important events
- changes in circumstances
- social history
- physical health
- mental health
- education
- training
- employment
- legal status
- placement history
- abuse
- offences.

A chronology is a factual document; it should not contain any opinions, judgements or analysis.

Summaries

Many long-term benefits can accrue if a worker gets into the habit of writing summaries regularly on a service user's file. A summary should be part of the recording process, not something which is done hurriedly when some sort of review is due to take place. Workers are likely to moan that adopting this habit creates even more work for them, but actually it probably could save time and more work in the long run. If a summary is written every three months as part of the process record it helps the worker to:

- be objective
- analyse and evaluate work undertaken in supervision sessions

- prepare chronologies

- write reports.

BEST PRACTICE POINTS

A summary should be an overview of:
- objectives, methodology, work undertaken, outcomes
- contact
- resources put in/how used
- new information gained from key individuals/organisations
- analysis of progress/failure i.e. things which are not working well
- service user's views
- suggested changes/modifications to ways of working
- objectives for next three months.

Suggested reading

Davies, M. (1993) 'Recognizing Abuse: An Assessment Tool for Nurses.' In P. Decalmer and F. Glendenning (eds) *The Mistreatment of Elderly People*. London: Sage.

Davies, M. (1997) 'Key Issues for Nursing: The Need to Challenge Practice.' In P. Decalmer and F. Glendenning (eds) *The Mistreatment of Elderly People*. 2nd edition. London: Sage.

Hartman, A. (1995) 'Diagrammatic assessment of family relationships.' *Families in Society* 76, 111–122.

Hartman, A. (1979) *Finding Families: An Ecological Approach to Family Assessment in Adoption*. Beverly Hills, California: Sage Publications.

McGoldrick, M., Gerson, R. and Petry, S. (2008) *Genograms: Assessment and Intervention*. 3rd edition. New York: W.W. Norton and Company.

McGoldrick, M. and Gerson, R. (1985) *Genograms in Family Assessment*. New York: W.W. Norton and Company.

Chapter 6

Evidential Requirements 1: Preserving and Presenting the Evidence

The word 'evidence' may be interpreted differently by each reader of this book. Social work students have to evidence their competence; police and prosecutors look for evidence to prove a crime has been committed. So why do we have to think about evidence in this book which is focusing on recording skills? The main reason is that if it is suspected that abuse is taking place, it is necessary to prove that it has happened and/or is continuing to happen. We cannot rely on gut feeling; workers have to look for signs and symptoms of abuse and be able to verify that such symptoms are not indicators of other conditions, illnesses, or situations. Some abuse cases will be worked on by adopting a criminal justice model, which will necessitate getting evidence for court. Even if a case is not going down the criminal justice route a welfare model may be adopted and civil proceedings can sometimes take place. In any of these situations written documents are going to be required, that is, to evidence what has been found. Hence it is necessary to look at some definitions of evidence and consider what police, crown prosecution lawyers and the courts require.

What is evidence?

DEFINITIONS OF EVIDENCE

- *information or signs indicating whether a belief or proposition is true or valid*
- *law information used to establish facts in a legal investigation or admissible as testimony in court.*

(Oxford English Dictionary)

In England and Wales the legal system has criminal law and civil law. What is required as proof is set by a different standard depending on the type of proceedings, namely, criminal or civil. In criminal cases the prosecution has to prove the case 'beyond all reasonable doubt'; that means if there is the slightest doubt at all about whether a person is guilty of committing the offence the finding has to be one of 'not guilty'. Civil proceedings work on a less rigid standard of proof – the 'balance of probabilities'. The standard here is that it is more likely to be true that the offence has been committed than not true, that is, working on a 50 per cent plus basis.

Most people have heard the terms 'hard evidence', 'supporting evidence', 'preponderance of evidence' but what do these words actually mean? All sorts of things could be evidence and here are some more words which might be associated with that word:

- factual
- real
- documentary
- written
- hearsay
- opinion
- expert

- statements
- objects
- exhibits
- behavioural
- circumstantial
- medical
- forensic.

Depending on what sort of job you have, you are likely to interpret the meaning of evidence differently. Before we explore in depth what types of written records could be used as evidence, it is important to look at the role of the Crown Prosecution Service (CPS), who are ultimately responsible for deciding whether a criminal case should proceed to court.

What the Crown Prosecution Service has to do

Both the police and the CPS come in for a lot of criticism from people who do not have any understanding of the legal system in the UK. There can be a lack of understanding why so few cases of abuse get to court. There can be an assumption that it is because the victim is not going to be a credible (i.e. good enough) witness. It is much more complicated than that and people need to understand that solicitors in the CPS have to adhere to *The Code for Crown Prosecutors* (CPS 2004). A police officer who has the lead for safeguarding adults talks about his own experiences of prosecutions:

Expert's experience and comment

We currently do about 200 investigations a year. The problem CPS has is they have to prove beyond all reasonable doubt in criminal cases. As a result of this a lot of the investigations which we currently undertake result in people receiving cautions. I would say out of 500 referrals 20–30 per cent are not criminal. Of the remainder, 10 per cent result in a positive outcome of either caution or charge. The majority of the cases have been care homes, community care agencies or supported living projects. Unfortunately cases involving family members as abusers have become more apparent in key areas such as financial abuse and neglect.

Police Officer

Crown Prosecutors make charging decisions in accordance with the Full Code Test, which has two stages:

> The first stage is consideration of evidence. If the case does not pass the evidential stage it must not go ahead no matter how important or serious it may be. If the case does pass the evidential stage, Crown Prosecutors must proceed to the second stage and decide if a prosecution is needed in the public interest. (CPS 2004, p.5)

It is not necessary to go into too much detail about these two stages, but any worker who keeps written records in their job needs to understand what the CPS has to do and why written records can be very important in the process. Regarding the evidential stage the code states:

> **5.2** Crown Prosecutors must be satisfied that there is enough evidence to provide a 'realistic prospect of conviction' against each defendant on each charge. They must consider whether the evidence can be used and is reliable. They must also consider what the defence case may be and how that is likely to affect the prosecution case.

> **5.3** A realistic prospect of conviction is an objective test. It means that a jury or a bench of magistrates, properly directed in accordance with the law, will be more likely than not to convict the defendant of the charge alleged. This is a separate test from the one that criminal courts themselves must apply. A jury or magistrates' court should only convict if it is sure of a defendant's guilt.

5.4 When deciding whether there is enough evidence to prosecute, Crown Prosecutors must consider whether the evidence can be used and is reliable. (CPS 2004, p.5)

Where there is a realistic possibility of securing a conviction the public interest test has to be undertaken:

5.8 Crown Prosecutors must balance factors for and against prosecution carefully and fairly. Public interest factors that can affect the decision to prosecute usually depend on the seriousness of the offence or the circumstances of the suspect. Some factors may increase the need to prosecute but others may suggest that another course of action would be better. (CPS 2004, p.8)

Finally there is just one more test which requires some explanation but is less likely to be the concern of the reader. However, it is often talked about at the same time as the tests already mentioned above.

6.2 The Threshold Test is applied to those cases in which it would not be appropriate to release a suspect on bail after charge, but the evidence to apply the Full Code Test is not yet available. (CPS 2004, p.12)

Before returning to the subject of written records and how they might be used as evidence it is useful to ponder on the following comment from a police officer. Although he is talking about social workers in particular, the difficulties he is talking about could apply to a lot of health and social care professionals:

Expert's experience and comment

Social workers need to see themselves as a professional witness; they are not going to court as a general member of the public. The fact that social workers appear scared at the prospect of going to court and are ill prepared means that they could potentially undermine the prosecution.

Police Officer

Geraldine Monaghan has a memory of what was said to a social worker in a child protection case:

Expert's experience and comment

Defence lawyer said to social worker, 'We don't want any anecdotal information' – meaning he did not consider the social worker's testimony to be 'evidence', which shows how a social worker's contribution can be seen.

Geraldine Monaghan

Records as evidence

There are many workers across the sectors who may not realise that the things they write down during the course of their daily work could be used as evidence in a court of law. If they have not been told this fact then how are they supposed to know? The list below shows some types of written records that are kept by workers in their organisations regarding service users; this list is certainly not exhaustive.

TYPES OF WRITTEN RECORDS

- referral
- assessments
- agreements
- contracts
- activity sheets
- daily record sheets
- inventory sheets
- care plans
- safeguarding/protection plans
- medical records
- medication records
- summaries
- chronologies
- genograms
- ecomaps
- bodymaps
- monitoring protocols

- memos
- letters
- forms
- accident/incident forms
- reports
- review documents
- minutes of meetings
- contact sheets (example of a running record)
- case records (example of a process record)
- notes
- messages (including e-mails)
- communication book
- diaries
- notebooks
- signing in and out book.

What many workers do not realise is that any of the above could be used as evidence in an abuse case. Other things which might not automatically spring to mind when thinking about records but in fact could also be crucial as evidence are:

- menus

- record of food/liquid intake

- medication chart

- bank statements

- savings accounts statements.

Organisations will also keep records related to staff, such as:

- personnel records

- training profiles

- supervision notes

- rotas.

These records will not be called for in every case which goes to court, but they could become evidence if they show how a person has presented or how they have been treated. Therefore, it is important that anything which is written down is done in a clear and concise way. If records are presented in an easy to understand way, then a solicitor in the CPS or a judge in a courtroom is going to take notice of what is produced as written evidence. If a record is illegible, full of waffle, or the meaning and point are unclear there is a real risk that it may be dismissed by a court, however important its content.

We shall now consider some of the documents which could be used as evidence and the dilemmas which arise for workers. It is important to say we shall not be going through every type of document that could be used as evidence; that would be an impossible task. We shall also be including comments from experts which will explain some of their own experiences but also give some practical advice. A good example is this comment from a police officer who has the lead for investigating abuse cases:

Expert's experience and comment

Recording? Care homes have been much better than social workers. They have forms for everything. At least they complete them – they don't always know why – but it is something. Big homes are too big, little ones are too small. Medium is best. Recent example a [large independent care provider] home where a complaint of neglect was made by a family member regarding failure to administer medication. This case was ultimately proved as a result of the records held within the home.

Police Officer

Geraldine Monaghan also has good advice to start any worker thinking:

Expert's experience and comment

Civil remedies – records will be required as evidence. The same is true in criminal proceedings. We should be writing the records with that in mind.

Geraldine Monaghan

Service user/case files

The main problem nowadays is that organisations have different systems for keeping service user case files; some keep paper files, others are paperless (i.e. only electronic files are kept), some keep both types of records. So inconsistency prevails. Whatever type of files are kept, a high standard of recording is required and it should be done regularly, namely, files should be kept up to date. This has been discussed at length in Chapter 4 and does not need to be repeated here. What does need to be emphasised is that all organisations need to have good recording systems which enable a worker to record consistently to a high standard. Training needs to be given to explain what needs to be recorded where and when: that is which sheets, forms or templates have to be used and in what circumstances. Training on record-keeping should be kept updated and be part of a rolling programme because of staff turnover and because it is a topic that needs to be kept at the forefront of workers' minds.

Notes

Note-taking is a skill which needs to be developed because it can facilitate the production of a good record. Notes help memory recall, but they can also provide crucial evidence. A term which all workers should become familiar with is 'contemporaneous notes,' that is, notes taken at the time of talking, disclosure, interviewing. Notes should be kept until it is as clear as it can be that they are no longer needed. Steve Kirkpatrick, a former police officer, talks about the importance of note-taking:

Expert's experience and comment

Courts do not tend to criticise if there is any kind of notes taken in some form. In my current role[1] there tends not to be any notes made at all when there is suspected abuse. This is due to inexperience and lack of training. I do not remember note-taking as part of any Safeguarding Vulnerable Adults training I have ever attended. I find that it is not habitual practice for care assistants to make notes or compile a duty statement. I always have to ask! This is not a criticism but stating a reality. The problem is that I might not be told until four days later and then it is not as fresh in their minds.

I dealt with an incident in my new role where a vulnerable adult had said something to a carer on the Sunday. The manager spoke to the carer on Monday morning and I then spoke to them on the Tuesday morning. During that time the 'place' where it occurred changed on each retelling and the event moved from being a routine one to a very intrusive assault. It is not possible to know with any certainty if this was because the event was imagined due to dementia or the recollection of exact words spoken were not correct. For example on the first telling of the event, the vulnerable adult might not have actually said where it had happened; the carer might have assumed it, then inadvertently said it as fact in the reporting of it to the manager. Write it down at the time! The exact words spoken! It helps for managers to be able to better analyse the information.

When I was later recounting this incident to a social services manager even I inadvertently misquoted what was said to me. When I revisited my notes which were made at the time of my interview with a service user I realised my mistake. Fortunately it did not take away anything material from the joint decision. So it is important to make any notes immediately after the incident or conversation, because time will interfere with our

1   Steve Kirkpatrick is currently Chief Executive of Gold Hill Care and previously was a Detective Inspector in the Thames Valley Police.

recollections. And it is important to read from your notes, not your own recollection of what you have written.

Steve Kirkpatrick

Another police officer in interview talked about his own practices when talking to victims of abuse and how his approach is very different. This particular officer regularly goes out with social workers to interview victims:

Expert's experience and comment
There is a massive reluctance to get pens out of their pockets and write things down. Going out on a joint visit to someone's home, I scribble away like mad; they just sit back and smile.

Police Officer

Notebooks

Many workers take notes in notebooks and then write up their notes on the service user file. However, it often comes up on training courses that some workers (e.g. home carers, care workers, support workers in the voluntary sector) do not carry even the smallest of notebooks with them whilst they are at work. It is important to do so because if a service user starts talking about something important (e.g. giving a disclosure about abuse) it is essential that some notes are taken. Notes that are taken at the time something is said or done are known as contemporaneous notes and as stated previously are important because they have to be submitted to the evidential test. Workers need to be clear that notes written up after an event are not contemporaneous notes. Therefore, any notes which may be needed as evidence should be torn out of a notebook and stored in a service user's file. A dilemma which arises here is that workers who are working in paperless offices are told that they cannot keep any paper. Consequently original notes are often scanned. Organisations really need to address their thinking on this and give guidance to workers about how and where crucial notes will be kept.

Expert's experience and comment
I know it's controversial, but I still think diaries are the best way or a notebook. If this is not preferred then on A4 lined paper. Date, time, place, exact words spoken or what injuries seen and

where exactly. Social Care Software packages are not generous in providing space to log any concerns of suspected abuse. They are not easy to access when you want to make a quick note. Keeping a small notebook on you, is a good idea. Wouldn't it be good if some had an icon button press which when you did it listed all the possible indicators to consider which might tend to suggest the vulnerable adult is being abused! Now that would be an information system worth having.

Steve Kirkpatrick

BEST PRACTICE POINTS

- Always carry a notebook and pen about your person when at work.
- Whenever you are told something important, make some notes to help you remember clearly later what was said. Make these notes at the time if you can, or as soon as possible afterwards.
- Keep notes until it is clear that they are no longer needed.

Messages

It all too easy to write a message for someone who is out of the office on a bit of paper that is just to hand. We have all been given messages like the one below which was written on a post-it sticker:

Example of bad message taking

Mrs Arthur rang again. Can you ring her before 2?
P.S Don't forget drink tonight after work – Kate's last day!

There is often inconsistency in how messages are taken within organisations. Workers and teams use different resources and methods to pass on messages:

- message pad (with or without a carbon copy)
- message book
- post-it stickers
- notepaper

- e-mails

- telephone answer machines

- faxes

- text messages

- voicemail.

Any message needs to be written down correctly (including messages taken off an answering machine or voicemail) and must include the following detail:

BEST PRACTICE POINTS
- date and time of call/visit
- name of caller/visitor and their position [check spelling, rather than relying on how names sound]
- telephone contact number/or address [read back to ensure these are noted correctly]
- who the message is for
- the message
- print name of person who took the message and job title
- signature of person taking message
- date and time person finished writing the message
- consider the best way to ensure the message is seen and acted upon promptly. It may be enough to e-mail it or leave a note in the recipient's mail basket. But consider what to do if the message is urgent or the recipient is going to be unavailable for some time.

As technology continues to develop, there is likely to be even more inconsistency and organisations must give clear guidance to their workers in a recording policy that should be reviewed regularly.

E-mails

It is very evident that workers deal with e-mail messages in very different ways. Some workers keep them all either in an Inbox which gets very full, or they create a special folder to store them in. Others cut and paste the message into a case record whilst some print the e-mails and keep them in a paper file. Workers need to check if their organisation does have guidance on archiving e-mails; such guidance also needs to state how long files are kept. Sometimes files can be deleted by the organisation's IT system after a certain time period without a worker knowing this is policy. Another problem can be when a worker leaves an organisation their name is automatically deleted from files and consequently it is not possible to know who wrote the original document.

KEY QUESTIONS

- Do you know if your organisation has a policy regarding e-mails and storage?
- Can you locate all incoming and outgoing e-mail on a given case?
- Is all e-mail attached to the case record?

Diaries

It is advisable for a worker to keep work and personal diaries separate. The main reason is that the work-related information in a diary belongs to the organisation which employs the worker. A manager (and senior management) has the right to read the diary at any time. The contents could also be shared with other professionals in certain circumstances (police, solicitors). If a worker leaves the employment of an organisation they should in fact leave their diary; few do even when it is stated in a recording policy, because there is a fear that the diary might be lost by the organisation. Electronic diaries are now used quite frequently by workers which in one way helps, but in another way means life has become more complex when it comes to archiving. Once again organisations should inform workers how long information is stored in electronic diaries.

Everyone uses their diary in a different way. Some workers will write the bare minimum, just entering appointments. Nevertheless, this is extremely useful because it is a record of when and where a worker has been or when things have been cancelled, so the entries can act as an aide memoire years later if necessary. Other workers write copiously in their diary, really using it like a notebook. However, non-emergency use of diaries for evidential note-taking should not be encouraged. Partly it may blur the boundary between the bare minimum information a diary is intended for and the fuller recording which really belongs elsewhere; partly it means that one ends up with confidential information about a number of service users in a single volume – unless the pages are torn out, which rather defeats the purpose.

Geraldine Monaghan explains an interesting experience her colleague Mark Pathak had which shows the value of keeping a detailed record of appointments within a diary:

Expert's experience and comment

At court one of two sisters with whom we had been working said (quite inaccurately) that Mark saw them both together to do Witness Support, Preparation & Profiling (WSP&P). Such an arrangement would have risked compromising them as witnesses and was contrary to the undertaking we had given the court. The only time Mark saw them together was the initial 'hello' meeting, accompanied by the Investigating Officer from Merseyside Police.

The quickest and most effective way for us to deal with this was for Mark to make a brief written statement outlining the arrangements made and attaching a photocopy of his diary entries for the relevant appointments. He was prepared to produce the original diary to the court if required.

It was accepted that the witness had made a mistake (flustered by Counsel!), so her evidence had not been compromised and could be heard.

Geraldine Monaghan

Victims' writing

We need to return to the importance of victims' writing being used as evidence, which has been mentioned briefly in earlier chapters (2 and 4). Many workers do not automatically ask whether a service user wants to contribute to their own record. This is an important issue to think about when dealing with victims of abuse. Some victims will have kept a record of what has happened to them when they have been living in an abusive situation. As technology has developed so quickly in recent years and people communicate by text and e-mail, we tend to forget that the older generations may communicate in more traditional ways, for example, writing proper letters, keeping diaries or journals. An older victim of abuse might have kept diaries or journals in the past, and may even have carried on doing so now.

This was true of a woman called Betty, who had lived in a domestic violence situation for 43 years before she left her husband. Betty had always written in a journal and catalogued the violence she had experienced. After leaving her husband, her youngest son started to abuse her financially. Betty continued to keep a journal; she wrote about her son taking advantage of her but also about the memories of the babies who had died due to the violence from her husband. Betty could talk and write very easily; she also wrote poetry to express her feelings. Other victims find it hard to articulate themselves verbally and may find writing or drawing an alternative way of telling their stories. Denise, who was a victim of child sexual abuse and domestic violence, is one such person. She kept a journal when she was attending a therapeutic support group for victims of abuse.

Extracts from Betty's journal and her poems have been published elsewhere as have the writings of Denise (Pritchard 2003; Pritchard and Sainsbury 2004). A few extracts are presented here to illustrate that a person may be able to write about their past history, but also how they are feeling on a day-to-day basis. Such writing can give a worker a clear insight into how someone is feeling and can be used therapeutically to work through issues with the victim. Jan, a survivor of child abuse and domestic violence, is currently working through the healing process. She is using writing from her past but also continues to write her thoughts and feelings down on a regular basis, which helps her to set objectives during the therapeutic sessions.

Creative writing can be used in court as evidence, but also can evidence what work has been undertaken with a person and which methods a worker has adopted.

Examples of victims' writing

Extracts from Betty's journal

Tuesday 1 August The day started slowly and the warden called as did [son] for the usual reason – money. He is talking about a change of jobs. I pray it will mean less visits.

Friday 11 August Certain days of the year are important for me to recall the dates of babies. I lost eight in all, but I do have 2 healthy sons.

Saturday 12 August Monday 12.08.68 I gave birth to a son MICHAEL 3LB 4OZ. I will never forget him. So today has me feeling sad.

Tuesday 15 August Another sad day my baby MICHAEL died 3 days old. I still ask why me. I had no visitors as usual. 1968 was not a good year for me; it was yet another memory. They called him 'little boxer' as he had a black eye.

Wednesday 23 August As days go [son] is calling in for his lunch at 1.00 pm and goodies for his snap; it never fails to amaze me. I admit I do worry about him and always will. A strange thing is I forgot what day it was and why the sun was at the back in a morning 5–10 pm.

Denise's written account of past abuse
BEING ABUSED FROM THE AGE OF 5 YEARS

When I was five years old I was abused physically, mentally and sexually. My dad used to tell me to get to bed all the time. He used to abuse and bully me, all the time. I was what was known as the black sheep of the family. I had three brothers and two sisters. My dad used to abuse me all the time, he used to make me stand on a sideboard and when mum came from town, on a Saturday, if I didn't tell her I was an Indian he would hit me bad. He has even hit me with a glass milk bottle, the abuse with dad carried on until I was around 17–18 years. Then came my stepdad. He married mum when I was 13 years old and had started to abuse me a few weeks later. I was in a children's home and was sexually abused, while I was either on holiday or I was on weekend leave. My mum was aware of this abuse, but I can understand why now she was afraid. She was beaten a lot of the time. I was abused by my stepfather. I had my son at 16 years old in April as I would have been 17 in June. I only got the chance to get into a proper relationship as my stepdad was sent to prison for armed robbery. But even from prison I was getting threats. When my stepdad did get released the abuse started again and did not stop until I was 24 years old. I never told anyone apart from my mum, who didn't believe me. How could mum not believe me when she was in the room some of the time? She too is full of crap. So my thoughts were if I can't be believed by my mum, who else would want to listen? I had three children to my stepdad. I wasn't allowed to talk to guys and if I did, I was beaten bad. He gave me black eyes, broken bones in my ankle and my nose was broken, I had cracked ribs. I was beaten once so badly. I crawled to a police station, but dared not go in, as he found me outside the police station he said if I told anyone he would kill my son and nothing or no-one was worth my son's life. My stepfather also at one time abused my son and my oldest daughter. My stepdad also once put a verse in the memory column, saying that my son had passed away. That's why I kept all my abuse to myself for 23 years. In my early years when I was 8 years old I was raped by a family friend, then raped again at 9 years old. I find it very hard to cope with all of this and tried to take my own life on many occasions.

In 1994 18 June I got married and I left him within 12 months. He was a drinker and started to hit me and I couldn't cope with it. Then in 1995 April 23 I met a man who I have lived with for 7 years. He too was a bully. I have had a broken nose in two places. He once tried to set me on fire while I was in bed. This was because he wasn't able to cope without a fag.

I have taken overdoses while being with this man. Some serious overdoses. On 14 December 2002 I took a massive overdose and I was on a life support machine. I left the hospital on 21 December. I couldn't stand to be in the same place as him and I ended up in Churchtown Psychiatric Unit, Trinity 2. I am still there and today is 7 February 2003. I am in the same house when I am on home leave. I hate this house and am going to be rehoused somewhere else. I want to make a new start and have a new life without any abuse in any form. I have been going to a group once a month, which is like a lifeline to me. The people who run it are called Jacki and Janice. Without the group I'd be buggered. I have special people in my life and they are there for me. I also have the staff to thank on the ward, as they have been an absolute godsend to me and all who are included in my ward round. The people who pretend to be your friend aren't worth the friendship, then there are the real friends who are there for you. My special friends are there for me, and the staff who are looking after me on the ward have done more for me than my family have, and now hopefully I can forget the past and look forward to the future.

Jan's feelings, thoughts, and targets

TURMOIL

Turmoil this is my mind, my thoughts a jumble, I cannot make any sense out of it, out of life.

Why am I here?

Who am I here for?

Who really wants or cares for me?

For many years my life has felt like an obstacle course, where the rules are changed or broken.

It's an ordeal, something to be got through, with no reward at the end.

Life events and experiences or observations and insights into the lives of others make me ask why I don't have the same things happen sometimes?

At work people I see daily with severe problems of illness or disease make me feel guilty for my feelings of despair.

Why do I feel like this?

Where do I find this elusive contentment?

Does it exist?

If it is true that I do deserve better then where do I find this?

How will I know if it finds me?

I HAVE TO:

Be more tolerant.

Be more trusting.

Be more accepting.

Allow individuality.

Avoid making comparisons.

Not take things personally.

Build self-confidence.

Be open.

Not bottle things up.

Always listen (and really hear).

Swallow my pride.

Apologise when wrong.

Avoid sulking.

Make sure things are out in the open (no secrets).

Never jump to conclusions.

Be forgiving.

Have patience.

Avoid taking charge.

Give and take.

Not drag up the past (My Mantra).

This chapter has considered why recording is important from a criminal justice point of view, that is, how records can be used as evidence. It has also discussed how records can evidence what workers do in their day-to-day practice of working with victims of abuse. We want to conclude this chapter with some anecdotal experience and advice from Steve Kirkpatrick and best practice guidance from David Hewitt, a lawyer who is very experienced in dealing with people with mental health problems. David's summary will lead us on to think in more detail about producing written records as evidence through the whole investigation process which is the focus of the next chapter.

Expert's experience and comment

Question: Have you any particular advice to give about recording and evidence?

I like to look at recording from a different angle, not just because of the Criminal Court ramifications. I think that anyone who works as a professional should keep good daily notes/diary entries, not just to assist any possible investigation, but to also protect themselves from criticism and litigation. Most of us are doing a splendid job, but when our work comes under scrutiny we are not easily able to justify or give a good account of the good work we have done. In both my careers from time to time my work has come under scrutiny, either because of unfounded allegations or because I have not done my job as well as I ought to have done.

I can think of one particular case in my police role where we had to release a man who had raped a woman, and after his release he went on to murder another woman. Although I had done nothing wrong, this case taught me a valuable lesson about record-keeping. My notes simply were not good enough. I had to give evidence in the Crown Court and the national spotlight was on me.

Question: What lessons did you learn from that experience?

Although I had a collection of documents consisting of witness statements, interview records and a write off report, I did not have a chronological log of my meeting with the prosecutor I had consulted with nor anything in writing from him of his decision not to charge. Nor did I have a running log of the investigation. It was after this that I started to keep copious records in hard-backed A4 books, the pages of which I numbered. I would use this book when I had face to face meetings or telephone conversations with key people concerning investigations. Also about this time I began a new role as Deputy Senior Investigating Officer within major incident rooms. One of my bosses used to dictate into a dictaphone a running log of the investigation, implications of the information gathered, various options of possible actions and new enquiries and corrections to current enquiries, and decisions as to ways forward. From him I developed this over the next few years and used to input these logs directly into a running word document; always resaving any additions with new dates and/or times in the title of the file, this leaving a proper audit trail which could be later scrutinised by a court or tribunal.

Ever since I have kept copious notes and diary entries going back to 1990 about most things I do. Thankfully this has held me in good stead when I have been on the receiving end of a couple of unfounded allegations during my police career.

Question: From your experience as a police officer, do you think professionals (socials workers, nurses, doctors) kept 'good enough' records? What sort of things were missing?

No notes at all – not mentioning other people working or present when something happened. Incidents need to be corroborated and to go back later. To expect people to remember things is not easy. Also missing dates, times, what part of the building the incident or event was witnessed. Workers need to be familiar with any frameworks such as validity statement analysis; this will help the credibility of the evidence of a vulnerable witness.

In turn then, look out and listen for anything which a witness says which tends to suggest that they are telling the truth. Before I was aware of the statement validity assessment points I am sure that I missed recording things a vulnerable witness said because I did not appreciate the significance of them. Once I had reflected on a seminar presented by Professor Gunter Konkhen, I started to record in my notes and witness statement phrases vulnerable adults were saying that suggested they were telling the truth.

The key points for consideration which tend to suggest that a witness maybe telling the truth are:

- contextual embedding
  - events are placed in time and location – victim describes that the crime occurred in a park at noon when the man was walking his dog
- descriptions of interactions
  - statements contain information that interlinks the alleged perpetrator and witness
- reproduction of conversation
  - specific dialogue, not summaries of what people said
- unexpected complications during the incident
- superfluous details
  - details that are non-essential to the allegation, such as a vulnerable adult describing that the perpetrator sneezed
- accurately reported details misunderstood
  - mentioning of details outside a person's scope of understanding
- self-deprecation – witness does not hide facts which show them in a bad light or even that they have done things wrong themselves
- accounts of subjective mental state
  - description of a change in a subject's feelings during the incident.

Steve Kirkpatrick

Expert's experience and comment
Record-keeping: a legal perspective

1. Good quality care often depends upon good quality notes. It is therefore essential for patients and clients that you make such notes, and it is a matter of courtesy to your professional colleagues.

2. In fact, the making of an adequate, contemporaneous record will usually be a requirement of professional practice, and the failure to do so a disciplinary offence.

3. This isn't, however, a counsel of perfection: only the most significant interventions will require the most significant notes.

4. For the most part, you should record (1) what you did; (2) why you did it and (3) the legal basis for doing it. (The last will often require discussion of the rules about capacity and consent or the **Mental Capacity Act 2005**.)

5. When making a recording, you should consider relevant professional standards, and also the requirements of your employer. You should, for example, take special care to identify any note that is not contemporaneous (in other words, not made at the time of the events it describes).

6. For most lawyers, however, and in most circumstances, the fact that an intervention **is** recorded is more important than the place **in which** it is recorded. Your employer might require that you make notes in a particular place, and if so, you should try to respect that requirement. Where, however, an adequate note has been recorded but in the wrong place, that might be a disciplinary issue, but it will be easier to defend than if no record was made at all.

7. In some cases – for example, where a patient is detained under the **Mental Health Act 1983** – the law itself requires that particular information be recorded in a particular place (such as a statutory form). If so, it will be difficult to defend an intervention that is not recorded in that place.

8. It is the intervention you make that is most important, and your recollection of that intervention.

9. It is sometimes said of an intervention that if it isn't recorded, it didn't happen. In my opinion, that is nonsense: I can remember my football team's last match all too clearly, even though I didn't make any notes about it. (We lost 1–2 at home, missed a penalty and had three men, including our manager, sent off.) Others have different opinions, of course, but most agree that a recording simply aids recollection; it is rarely a substitute for it.

10. That isn't, of course, the whole story. You may, if you are content to do so, rely solely upon your own recollection of an intervention, but in the absence of a written record, you should be prepared for the accuracy of that recollection to be challenged.

11. When preparing a statement or report, you should make sure, before putting pen to paper (or finger to keyboard), that you know precisely what is expected of you. A statement for the coroner is very different from a report to a tribunal or in court proceedings: different issues are in play and different judicial approaches will be taken. (You should take special care if you are not going to seek formal advice from a lawyer.)

12. The same applies if you have been asked to prepare an independent opinion in connection with legal proceedings. In that situation, you should be very clear about what you are being asked to consider and by whom. You will need to know the issues in the case and how you will be expected to report your views. Ultimately, of course, your duty will be to the court in which those views will be aired, not to any particular party (even the one that will be responsible for your fee).

13. Speaking of inquests: you should try to retain control of any statements for the coroner. Those taken by the police, for example, are often unhelpful and do not acknowledge the clinical or professional realities of a case. It is usually better, even though it might take a little longer, to prepare your statement yourself. If the police (for example) have prepared a statement for you, you might wish to consider submitting a supplemental statement, setting out everything you are able to say about the issues in the case and putting it into its proper context.

14. Whatever you write, try to keep to the relevant issues. Any general summary need only be brief. In most cases, one or two paragraphs should suffice (although in more complex cases, a page or two might be more appropriate).

15. Bear in mind those who are likely to read what you write. For the most part, they will be laymen, so you should explain any technical terms and in the case of an acronym, write it out in full the first time you use it.

16. It may seem trite (or even offensive) to say so, but you should take care over spellings, grammar and syntax, over technical terms and dates, and also over the names of those involved. In inquests, for example, I have read too many statements for the coroner in which the name of the deceased is misspelt or even wholly incorrect. That does not create a good impression.

17. Wherever possible, you should have your own (and your colleagues') notes available when you are preparing a statement. You might wish to expand upon, or even to contradict, contemporaneous recordings, but where you do so, you should explain why.

18. If there is a discrepancy between the notes and a statement, or between your evidence and that of another practitioner, you should ask whether it can be explained or the disparate versions reconciled. If not, you should expect to be challenged.

19. You should not, however, permit simple human errors throw you: the fact that two nurses disagree by ten minutes as to the time a dose of medication was given doesn't mean the dose wasn't given at all. (If they disagree not by ten minutes but by ten hours, that is a rather different matter.)

20. Keep a copy of whatever you write and do not assume that your employer will do the same. Your copy statement will enable you to refresh your memory before giving evidence. In some courts, you will be able to take it into the witness box with you, and in some cases it will even stand as your formal evidence (and you will simply be asked questions about it).

21. It is not just statements that practitioners – or, more often, their employers – should retain. In some cases, there can be an issue not just about the intervention recorded, but about the way it has been recorded. It might be suggested, for example, that the witness did not write an entry s/he claims to have written, or there might be doubt about precisely what has been written. In that situation, all concerned might need to have access to the original notes. For that reason, individuals or organisations that dispose of original notes do so at their peril (whether or not they retain paper or electronic copies).

22. Assiduous record-keeping is not without its dangers, however, as was made clear in **M v East London NHS Foundation Trust**, which came before Mr Justice Burton in the High Court in February 2009.[2] This was a mental health case in which the main issue was whether a patient's 'nearest relative' had told a social worker that he objected to the patient being detained in hospital. The judge found that the man **had** objected (and that as result, the patient's subsequent detention was unlawful), and he said he had felt able to do so largely because of the social worker's own 'impressive' note of the conversation.

David Hewitt

Suggested reading

Crown Prosecution Service (2004) *The Code for Crown Prosecutors.* London: CPS.
Check if your organisation has a policy on recording.

---

2   High Court (Queen's Bench Division), Mr Justice Burton, 11 February 2009, CO/1065/2009
     – see, in particular, paragraphs 17, 20 & 21.

Chapter 7

Evidential Requirements 2: Pre-alert to Case Conference

In this chapter we want to start looking at the recording which may need to be undertaken during the different stages of safeguarding adults work. We feel this will give a clear structure to the reader. The stages can be divided into:

- before an alert – when abuse is suspected or alleged
- making an alert
- investigation
- post-investigation.

The chapter will look at the situation before and during an investigation. Minute-taking in strategy meetings and case conferences will be touched on briefly here, but given in-depth attention in Chapter 9; just as the development of safeguarding plans will be given the attention they deserve in Chapter 8.

Suspecting abuse

We have already acknowledged earlier in the book that it can be a common occurrence for a worker to have a 'gut-feeling' that something is wrong; maybe that abuse is occurring. Workers are often scared to verbalise it, never mind write it down. It is important to emphasise to all workers that it is vital to record anything that makes one suspect that abuse is occurring. Training courses should ensure that workers understand that changes in behaviour, lifestyle and attitude can be indicators of abuse. Therefore, any change which a worker may pick up on – no matter how small – must be recorded. Sometimes it can take years to prove that abuse is happening; in such cases if notes have been made at an earlier point in time these can be used at a later date.

Workers will be reading this book who work in different settings, and their organisations will have different formats for recording. Some will record on a service user file in their case notes; other may have a specific form to complete after they have undertaken a visit. Whatever documentation is being used, any observations about changes should be written up as soon as possible with the time and date of the observations recorded.

In situations where notes are kept in the service user's home, workers should be careful not to record on a document which could be accessed by the alleged abuser. In the following case example the worker inadvertently put herself at risk of harm.

Case example of bad practice

Tessa was a domiciliary care worker who had been supporting Hettie regularly for over a year. Hettie lived with her son, Malcolm. Hettie repeatedly had a lot of bruising but had told Tessa she falls over a lot because of an ear imbalance problem she has always had. Tessa talked to her manager about her concerns and was told, 'to monitor carefully, write everything down and use bodymaps.' Having been told this, Tess did complete bodymaps which she left in Hettie's notes and were kept in the sideboard; but on one occasion she also wrote:

> 9.1.09 Have completed another bodymap like I've been told to because I really do think Malcolm is hitting his Mum. She's too frightened to say anything.

It never occurred to Tessa that Malcolm might see what she had written and he could have attacked her.

Learning point
When there is a situation whereby a suspected abuser may access a victim's notes, recording should be kept elsewhere, for example, back in the office.

Best practice
In this case Tessa should have tried to talk to Hettie in the first instance about her concerns. If this did not lead to Hettie disclosing the abuse, but Tessa continued to be concerned then the following should have happened:
- Tessa should record the conversation (including the date and time) she had with Hettie but she should not leave those notes in Hettie's house.

- Tessa should talk to her line manager, who should record the discussion.
- If the line manager was concerned about the situation she or he should make an alert to adult social care.
- The alert should be recorded in the agency's files, on an alerter form (if there is one in the local safeguarding adults policy) and/or an additional report should be written.

Receiving a disclosure

It is not unusual for a worker to receive a disclosure when it is least expected; commonly when doing something intimate like bathing, toileting or dressing someone. It is important that notes are taken at the time, that is, contemporaneous notes. Workers can feel uncomfortable about doing this, but it is important that they always carry a little notebook about their person. When this is discussed on training courses workers can get the idea that you stop anything you are doing immediately and start writing everything down. This is why they feel it could be deemed very rude. It is important to understand that notes can be taken in a sensitive way. If a worker explains their reasons for note-taking, this gives a positive message to the service user that what is being said is being taken seriously, namely, the person is being listened to. As soon as someone starts giving a disclosure, it is important to be aware of the time and for the worker to remind the person about the limits of confidentiality. Services users can feel 'betrayed' in situations where they give a disclosure after which the worker says they must report this to their line manager (see Pritchard 2000). This is why all workers should revisit the issue of confidentiality regularly when there is an ongoing working relationship.

BEST PRACTICE POINTS
- Explain about confidentiality and the need to report any concerns.
- Listen to the disclosure without interruption if possible.

- Say that some notes will be taken, but in addition explain *why* this is. A worker should say that they are taking what is being said very seriously and in order to make sure they remember things correctly they are going to jot down a few notes. This usually reassures the service user. It is absolutely fine to share those notes with the person.
- Notes should be as full as possible, but a worker should not feel they have to take a verbatim note.
- Keep the original notes.
- As soon as possible afterwards, write up what happened on the service user's file, namely, what led up to the disclosure, what was said and what action followed.

Making an alert

A worker should always report a disclosure or incident to their line manager as soon as possible. This sometimes has to happen by telephone contact, but ideally a worker and manager should meet face-to-face to discuss a disclosure which has been given. In other situations a worker may be voicing their concerns (talking about their gut-feeling) in an informal discussion with their manager. Whatever the situation a manager should always record the conversation which takes place between themselves and a worker. Exercise 7.1 has been designed to help managers think about questions they might ask a worker, to gain further information from them before deciding whether to make an alert or not. It is important for managers to ask the right questions and not to lead the worker. Many workers are scared of 'getting it wrong' and may be reticent in voicing their concerns. The main objective is for the manager to be able to make a good quality alert should that become necessary.

EXERCISE 7.1

MANAGERS HELPING WORKERS TO VOICE A CONCERN OR MAKE AN ALERT

OBJECTIVE
To help managers think about what questions they need to ask a worker (without contaminating evidence) who has a suspicion that abuse is happening, received a disclosure or has witnessed an incident.

PARTICIPANTS
To work in small groups of 3 or 4.

EQUIPMENT
Flipchart paper and pens.
Copies of Handout 7.1 with case studies.

TIME
15 minutes in groups; feedback – 10 minutes per group.

TASK

1. A group will work on just one scenario.

2. Participants are asked to imagine that a worker is coming to them as their line manager and verbalises to them what is written in the case scenario.

3. Participants will write on the flipchart: (i) questions they would ask the worker in order to get more information from the worker; (ii) subject areas they need to raise with the worker.

4. Participants will then discuss what they would do next, that is, would they make an alert at this point? If not, what would the justification be for this decision and what would they do instead? These decisions should be written on the flipchart sheet as though recording on a service user file.

FEEDBACK

1. The trainer will give everyone time to read the other scenarios on Handout 7.1.

2. Each group will feedback their work and the other groups will be asked to comment.

Handout for Exercise 7.1

1. Mr Buckley is the primary carer for his wife, Patricia, who has Alzheimer's disease. Patricia likes to walk around the house a lot and constantly wants to go upstairs which her husband discourages as he 'likes to keep an eye on her at all times.' Mr Buckley tells a home care worker that as he gets so tired sometimes with constantly 'having to watch her,' he locks her in the lounge. He also says he does this every night when he goes out for a drink to the local pub. His says it is 'the only time I get to myself.'

2. Sonia, who has moderate learning disabilities, is in hospital because she has got to have her wisdom teeth out. She has been chatting to one nurse in particular who she has taking a liking to – Jade Crook. During one conversation Sonia tells Jade that she does not like living at home because her parents are 'cruel' to her. When Jade asks her what she means Sonia says that both her father and mother hit her, and when she is 'bad' they do not feed her. Jade goes to the Ward Manager to talk about what Sonia has said.

3. Leon is a support worker in a voluntary organisation which works with people with mental health problems. During the past month Leon has been supporting Helen, aged 24, who experiences depression and severe anxiety. Helen lives with her father; her mother died two year ago. Helen discloses to Leon that her father has sexually abused her since she was 5 years old and the abuse is continuing. She says she is terrified of her father and his friends who he brings into the house, but does not want Leon to tell anyone. Leon has told Helen he must talk to his manager about this.

4. Care workers have been increasingly concerned about Edward (a 70-year-old man with dementia), whose behaviour has become more challenging towards male service users of the day centre. He had previously been verbally aggressive to both service users and members of staff and nothing much had been done to address this; no risk assessment had been undertaken. More recently he has hit some service users (men only, never women) and he has also thrown objects at them. One care worker now comes to the day centre manager to discuss her concerns.

5. Travis is 19 years of age and has just started to work for a voluntary organisation which provides supported accommodation for adults with learning disabilities. Travis is working night shifts in a house where there are four young men with severe learning disabilities. During his induction period he is working alongside Mike. In a supervision session Travis tells his manager that Mike brings in pornographic DVDs which he makes the service users watch; he also forces them to drink cans of beer which he brings in as well. When Travis questioned whether this was right Mike had said, 'I've worked here 5 years and know how to handle them to get a quiet shift.'

6. Ella is a community nurse and has just moved to a new city. Today she has been asked to administer an injection to a female patient, Mrs Jackson, in a care home. As soon as she entered the home Ella was aware of the stench of urine; she commented on this to a care worker who said one of the residents 'has just had an accident.' She was told Mrs Jackson was in the dayroom and that it would be alright to give the injection in there: Ella insisted on taking Mrs Jackson to the medical room, which was very dirty and full of empty boxes. Ella noticed that other residents she saw during her visit were very unkempt and seemed reluctant to engage in any conversation with her. On leaving the care home, Ella telephones her line manager.

It is really important that an alert is made properly; it can be done verbally but in addition there must be written documentation. One police officer who has lead responsibility for safeguarding adults investigations has described his local adult social care department as an 'archaic dinosaur' and explains how inefficient workers are at making alerts.

Expert's experience and comment

All social workers do is update computers then do a referral by making a telephone call to me; then they think that is it they don't have to do anymore. So I set up a referral system. E-mail referral system – just one mailbox – vulnerable adults inbox. In case something happens to me – I get run over by a bus, have an accident – referrals will be picked up by other officers in the office team. Once I set this up some [adult social care teams] stopped making referrals completely... I am constantly frustrated...except for some individual teams and their good managers. I deal with 10 teams which include adult social care, mental health and hospital trusts. I would say only two are any good.

Police Officer

During the course of the interview this same police officer talked about how his force's commitment to safeguarding adults and how specific computer systems have been developed to identify adults at risk:

Expert's experience and comment

We have a new Chief Constable who takes vulnerability – children and adults – very seriously. We have a new computer system on the division for all vulnerable adults. It shows agreed actions; updates addresses; says why they are vulnerable for example through own choice – frailty – other people; crimes which have happened; relevant parties; people providing support. Typical people on the system – those with mental health problems; suicidal people; people who do not understand their own vulnerability – victims of distraction burglaries. When an address is pulled up all the details come up with it.

Police Officer

The following checklist should help all managers and workers across the sectors to make better alerts:

CHECKLIST: RECORDING ALERTS

Have you:
- kept your contemporaneous notes?
- recorded on the service user's file?
- completed an alerter form (if required) or written a full report?

Things to think about when writing a fuller report:
- categories of abuse which are being alleged/suspected
- details of the alleged victim
- details of the alleged abuser
- abuse: time, place, frequency
- witnesses
- evidence
- capacity
- explanation by worker to service user re reporting/procedures
- consent to share information
- actions taken.

Receiving an alert

Once again there is a need to say that practices can differ when alerts are received by an adult social care department. A policy may say that an alert should come through to a central referral system or in some areas particular teams still have a traditional duty system which will accept the alert. If a worker is already involved with the alleged victim then sometimes that worker will be contacted direct. Whichever way the alert comes through, notes must be taken at the time and the required alert/ referral form completed. The minimum amount of information which should be recorded should include:

- alleged victim (e.g name, address, date of birth)
- alleged abuser (e.g name, address, date of birth)

- relevant details about the alleged victim and abuser (e.g. capacity issues, physical/mental problems, their relationship, housing situation)

- detail about the concern/ suspicion/allegation/incident (include dates/times/places where possible)

- alleged category(ies) of abuse

- other workers/agencies involved

- confirmation that the service user knows the alert is being made.

Expert's experience and comment

Evidence from the first person to receive a complaint is critical. They should accurately record what the complaint is and very importantly the demeanour and condition of the complainant (distressed, crying, dishevelled clothing, visible injuries etc.). What the complainant says is also important as in some cases what is said to another person (e.g. naming someone as having committed a particular act) can be repeated by the person to whom it is said as evidence in court. (This would usually be regarded as inadmissible under the hearsay rule but can be admitted at the discretion of the judge in sexual offences.)

Objects or clothing found at a scene should also be noted (but not touched) as should visible means of entry/exit by a possible offender. The sooner all these sorts of observations are recorded the more likely they are to be accepted as correct at court.

Roger Vickers

A worker who has taken an alert would normally then go to a manager to discuss it further. Sometimes where there is a central referral system the alert may be faxed through to a manager or team.

BEST PRACTICE POINTS

- Managers must also take notes of any telephone conversations or face-to-face discussions they may have.
- The date, time and duration of such communications must be recorded.

All managers will have their own preferences for recording. Some managers record in an A4 hardback notebook which they carry around with them all the time. Others will have a special 'safeguarding' or 'abuse' book. The only problem with this is that sometimes it may be necessary to rip out the notes and place them elsewhere, for example on a service user file. Because of this some managers prefer to carry a pad of A4 paper or have paper in a lever arch file. If notes from different cases are kept together it can be difficult to find something when you need it. Other managers prefer to type onto the computer as they are talking. Again the emphasis here is that contemporaneous notes should be taken in some format.

Managers can learn from a police officer who explained in interview how he has developed his own system for note-taking and recording, rather than using the traditional pocket book which police officers are expected to use.

Expert's experience and comment

A pocket book has serial numbers. Not functional for what I do. An investigating officers' day book is A4 – has 20 or 40 pages. No serial numbers. Not specific to each individual. It has other cases in it, so all that would have to go to Court. I use an A4 pad, put date and title (e.g. home visit, strategy meeting or whatever) at the top and page number. I rip the pages out and put them in a folder I have for each case. When closed it is stored in a banner box which is under my desk – it's ongoing. I have a banner box for each year. The year is written on the box, sealed and put in a store room.

Police Officer

Strategy meeting

After receiving an alert a manager has to decide whether to convene a strategy meeting or not. A strategy meeting can take place on the telephone or it can be a sit down meeting. Whatever format it takes there must be a written record of it. It is important to note that some safeguarding adults policies do have a template for recording the decisions of strategy meetings.

In emergencies, that is, where the alleged victim is deemed to be in immediate danger, the manager may speak to colleagues in the police, Care Quality Commission or other key individuals. As stated already, notes should be taken during these conversations and retained. When a strategy meeting is conducted in this way eventually the manager must write up a summary of the discussions and state clearly the decisions made, as these will form the minutes of the telephone strategy meeting.

Sometimes a strategy meeting is conducted very informally, that is, it is just a discussion between a worker and a manager. The same guidance applies – notes must be taken during the discussion and decisions formally written up and placed on the alleged victim's file. Where a strategy meeting is convened as a formal meeting, then minutes should be taken properly and this is the subject of Chapter 9.

BEST PRACTICE POINTS

- No matter how a strategy meeting is conducted, a record must be kept of what was said and the decisions made.
- If the strategy meeting is conducted on the telephone, the manager leading the conversations must take notes and then write a summary which will act as minutes.
- If the strategy meeting is a formal sit down meeting, minutes should be taken by a proper minute-taker.

However, in some areas they are not always convened as they should be. This is an ongoing problem for a police officer in his local area.

Expert's experience and comment

One of the greatest problems I have is strategy meetings not being minuted. I have a case example: financial abuse of an older person. At the strategy meeting there was me, the responsible manager, two social workers. The relative who reported it did not live near; in fact [lived] a long long way away. It was clear cut, good information from her. I was the only one who took notes during the meeting. I did it the way I always do it – mind mapping. I make a list of bullet points. Branches off from key words. I did what I had to do after the meeting and then there was a separate issue that arose later. The relative made a complaint about a social care agency. She had read the local vulnerable adults policy and procedure and made a complaint because she felt it had not been dealt with properly. I was asked for my notes from the strategy meeting because they were the *only record there was. The complaint was upheld because of my notes; procedures had not been followed.*

Police Officer

Strategy meetings can be complex and some difficult decisions have to be made. As we have said consistently in previous chapters, it is not good enough just to record a decision; there needs to be some explanation regarding how that decision was reached. Below is a summary of some of the key questions which need to be raised in a strategy meeting, and should also help the appointed investigating officers to prepare and plan their interviews:

KEY QUESTIONS

- Does the safeguarding adults policy and procedures need to be implemented?
- Is the alleged victim in immediate danger of harm? (risk assessment).
- Is a place of safety needed?
- Should there be a joint investigation – if so, which agencies will work together?
- Who will interview the alleged victim, that is, be investigating officers?
- When and where should the interview take place?
- Does the alleged victim have special needs?
- Are special measures required?
- Who else might need to be interviewed?
- When and where should these interviews take place?

With his extensive experience gained over years Roger Vickers is able to give the following advice:

Expert's experience and coment

Strategy meetings and case conferences reports are often poor. I have seen strategy meeting reports that just list he said, she said etc. I have seen very few (in fact none) that clearly cover the following areas:

- identify the individual circumstances and just what the safeguarding issue is

- given this, which organisation should lead and why (i.e. criminal allegation: police)
- which other organisations should contribute to the investigation
- the identity of representatives or, if not, who will nominate
- what information needs to be gathered
- how it will be gathered
- how organisations will co-operate to do this
- investigation time scales
- care for other service users
- care for staff involved
- media strategy.

Roger Vickers

Investigations

Investigating possible cases of adult abuse can be done in a variety of ways and circumstances. Sometimes the police will be involved, at other times they will not. If a criminal investigation is to take place, the police officers involved will be very clear about how they want to proceed with the job. It is evident that some police officers will interview alongside other professionals; others will not. In some cases the police will not have any involvement; then either one or two workers may be appointed to investigate. We do not intend to discuss every possible circumstance; our aim is to consider what records need to be kept. A fundamental problem is that workers who have never been memorandum trained under old child protection procedures or have not had the opportunity to attend an *Achieving Best Evidence* training programme may not know (and are not told by their managers) what documentation is crucial to an investigation. Workers need to be vigilant about keeping good records of all contact (telephone conversations, visits, interviews, discussions, meetings), which can be achieved by being rigorous about note-taking and writing up records as soon as possible, and by storing and archiving notes (by whichever chosen method – paper, scanning etc.).

Interviewing to gather evidence is very different from assessing people to meet their needs. Assessment skills do not become redundant; they can be utilised, but the way of questioning is very different. If proper specialised training has not been given, then a worker can unwittingly ask leading questions and contaminate evidence. Therefore it is important to prepare. When Steve Kirkpatrick, a former police Detective Inspector, was asked what advice he would give to inexperienced workers about writing up interviews, part of his response was about the questions used in interview:

Expert's experience and comment

This may sound strange, but the best advice I can give is to make notes beforehand in bullet points. So if you are going into an interview situation use your bullet points and make it clear that you prepared them beforehand. This kind of practice helps to enhance professionalism and credibility as a witness. What you are saying are words to the effect of: 'I do this kind of thing all the time in my work. This is always the kind of approach I adopt when I have to interview someone. I do this so I ensure I always ask open questions and do not put any thoughts or ideas into the head of the person I am interviewing.' It also helps to provide structure to what you are going to do and means you don't have to do so much writing – you have already done it. If you don't use any particular points, then cross them out during the meeting or make notes alongside them. Leaving large margins is useful for this. It also makes your notes appear genuine, which of course they are.

Steve Kirkpatrick

The exercise opposite has been published elsewhere (Pritchard 2007) but it is useful to include it here as it will help workers to practise developing and writing down questions.

EXERCISE 7.2

PREPARING FOR AN INVESTIGATION

OBJECTIVE
To train participants on how to prepare for an interview by using a definite structure.

PARTICIPANTS
In small groups.

EQUIPMENT
Flipchart paper and pens.
Copies of Handout 7.2.
Case studies – see Note for Trainer below.

TIME
Half day training session (about three hours).

TASK

1. Each group is given a different case study plus a copy of Handout 7.2.

2. Participants work through the tasks listed on Handout 7.2.

FEEDBACK

1. One case study is taken at a time. Each group will feedback their work.

2. The other participants will then comment on the questions which have been developed. Discussion should be encouraged around whether the questions are appropriate or leading. Participants are also encouraged to put forward other questions.

NOTE:
Managers or trainers will need to prepare case studies for this exercise or they may ask workers to use cases they have worked on previously for materials. However, if more case studies are needed a trainer may want to use case studies presented in *Becoming A Trainer in Adult Abuse Work* (Pritchard 2001); there are 20 in total. Case studies can also be found in *Working with Elder Abuse* (Pritchard 1996) and *Working with Adult Abuse* (Pritchard 2007).

✓

Handout for Exercise 7.2

1. Initial thoughts

- Remember about the concept of writing the script. Write down what you first thought after reading the case study.

2. What do you know already?

- List facts.

3. What do you need to find out?

- Before interview – is there anyone you need to contact for information?

- During the interview – list facts and information you need to obtain from the victim (i.e. the subject areas you hope the victim is going to talk about voluntarily) without being led during the free narrative part of the interview. If the subject areas and information are not given naturally, then it will be necessary to ask (non-leading) questions. Focusing on subject areas first will facilitate developing good questions as required in the next stage of the exercise.

4. Make a list of questions

- Take one subject area at a time and develop questions.

- These do not have to be in any order initially.

- Write each question in sentence form, that is, exactly how you would ask it.

- Cover all the subject areas listed under number three above.

- Begin with non-leading questions; you may have to go to closed questions eventually.

- When you have finished put the questions in order.

Taking notes during an interview

It is absolutely imperative that when conducting an interview written notes are taken. Even during a video interview a police officer in the monitoring room will be taking some notes. When other workers are acting as investigating officers best practice would indicate that two individuals are needed, because it is incredibly hard to focus on interviewing well (which involves questioning, observing, analysing, thinking ahead, constructing) and to take notes at the same time. Therefore, one worker should take the lead in order to ask questions, the second person should be taking notes and observing. The contemporaneous notes which are taken should be kept, even when the interview is written up formally. Significant times, not just the date, should be included in the notes, for example:

- when the interview started

- any breaks taken

- times of any particular observations, for example when the interviewee started crying

- when the interview finished.

Many workers say it is harder to take notes during an interview than to be the interviewer. This is because ideally the notes should be a verbatim account, that is, record word for word what is said. None of us are super human and many investigating officers will not have been on a speed writing course. Therefore, it is necessary to try to develop your own form of note-taking. Some of the tips given to minute-takers in Chapter 9 will be relevant to anyone who has the task of taking notes during an interview. However, it is important to think about:

BEST PRACTICE POINTS

- Have plenty of paper available and spare pens.
- Insert page numbers.
- Allocate initials to people present.
- Have margins on both the right and left of the sheet of paper. Decide which margins will be used for recording:
  - the speaker
  - times
  - observations.
- Put a signature and job title at the bottom of the notes.

A clear explanation of why notes are being taken should be given to the adult at the beginning of the interview; namely, that it is to enable the interviewer(s) to write a true account of what is being said and done during the interaction between the interviewer(s) and interviewee. There is nothing wrong with showing the notes to the person if they request this during the interview. It often helps a victim to know that what they are saying is being taken seriously.

After interview

If there are two investigating officers present at interview they should debrief each other, which will include going through the notes taken. The reality is that often the workers are feeling emotionally drained and very tired after an interview, but it is important to go through the notes if only quickly and then come back to them when the interview is going to be written up on the service user's file. Historically, in the child protection field workers have always been told it is best practice to write up an interview within 48 hours; the same guidance should be applied to recording interviews in safeguarding adults work. During the course of an investigation there could be a number of people interviewed. In fact in some cases there could be a massive number, for example, when there are large number of possible victims in a care home – both residents and the whole staff group may have to be interviewed. It is important to get individual interviews written up as soon as possible so the interviews do not become muddled in the workers' minds. Yet another reason for supporting the argument that there should always be two investigating officers.

BEST PRACTICE POINTS

You should always try to write up a disclosure or interview as soon as possible after the event has occurred.

- *Preparation* is the key – think before you write.
- You need to have *structure* – a beginning, middle and end and *relevant content*. A fundamental starting point is to ask the question – what is the purpose of the record/report?
- Remember to differentiate between *fact, opinion* and *hearsay*.

Below is a list of things you should think about before you start recording in a service user's case file or when preparing a report for a case conference:

- date, time, duration, location, people present at disclosure/ interview
- alleged victim's basic details
- alleged abuser's basic details (including relationship, if any, to the victim)
- alleged/possible types of abuse
- relevant background information/social history
- confidentiality – explanation to victim
- capacity
- consent
- sharing information – agreement of victim
- people involved with victim/abuser– agencies, family, friends, etc.
- liaison with other professionals, workers, agencies
- victim's account
- incident(s) – date, time, frequency, duration, location, triggers, detail of what happened
- before, during, after incident(s) – what was said/done
- victim's feelings/wishes – at time of abuse and at disclosure/ interview
- use of quotes
- observations
- recording of injuries, for example, bodymaps
- medical examination
- use of monitoring tools/protocols
- assessment of risk of significant harm
- actions taken
- agreements made with victim
- decision-making (including explanation of reasons for decisions taken)
- professional opinion
- work to be done
- name, job title, signature. date and time written record completed.

Case conferences

When there has been a formal investigation, then the findings of the investigating officers should be presented formally to a case conference, which should be convened to the same high standards we have come to expect in the child protection field. Sadly, this does not happen in some areas where the conference is conducted in a very casual way and participants can be unsure of the purpose of the meeting or why they have been invited to attend. Safeguarding adults polices should state clearly the objectives of a case conference which are to:

- share information in a multi-disciplinary forum

- determine on the balance of probabilities whether abuse has happened

- assess the risk of harm for the future

- make decisions and recommendations in the form of a protection plan.

Best practice requires that everyone attending a case conference should bring a written report. In some areas it is still only the investigating officers that produce a report. If everyone is required to submit a report there will eventually be consistency in practice, and this will help the risk assessment which needs to be undertaken (see Chapter 8). A policy and procedure document should state clearly what is required in such a report; some contain a pro-forma. The argument against a pro-forma is that it is too prescriptive, especially when it is in an electronic format. There needs to be room for the author of a report to be creative, because every case will be different. It is important not to allow a pro-forma to prevent important detail about the circumstances of the individual case being included. However, some possible subject headings which may be relevant to all cases are as follows:

- confidentiality – all reports must be marked confidential

- name of alleged victim and details (date of birth; address)

- name of alleged abuser and details (date of birth; address)

- the alert

- alleged categories of abuse

- strategy meeting: date and recommendations

- how the investigation was conducted

- interviews conducted

- evidence collected

- views/wishes of the victim

- opinion about whether abuse has been substantiated, not substantiated, inconclusive, with reasons

- recommendations.

For other workers who are not the investigating officers or for anyone who is inexperienced in writing reports, the following list of questions might help the planning process:

KEY QUESTIONS

- What do you know about the service user and his or her situation which is relevant to the conference?
- What information do you need to present? (facts).
- How will you present this information?
- Have you been using any monitoring tools? (evidence).
- What do you want to say? (opinion).
- Whose views are you representing (e.g. yours, the service user's, the agency's?).
- Is there anything else you need to do/find out before the conference?
- What will you put in a written report? (summary/conclusion).

The questions above should help a worker in planning to write a report, but some thought also needs to be given to what needs to be achieved within the contents of the report. The report should always be:

- *service user focused*: events and factors impacting on the victim; his or her account, experience, views, wishes and feelings

- *inter-agency based*: relevant and factual information collected from appropriate agencies, and attributed

- *factual*: include information which has been verified

- *accessible*: use plain language so the report can be easily understood

- *comprehensive*: includes all views not just those of the report writer

- *consistent*: all workers should write in the same format for case conferences

- *accurate*: cite all sources used to gather evidence and information

- *up to date/current*: the writer should not rely on old/out of date information

- *balanced*: this is really important. Of course a report for case conference or court needs to make clear and explicit how serious the concern and risk are, and to persuade other professionals or a judge to take action. However, this essentially negative message must be balanced by positives, for example the positive aspects of the relationship which gives cause for concern, or any protective factors. There are three reasons why it is crucial that reports achieve balance in this way:

  1. The report writer has a duty to the court, conference, etc. to give a full picture and not be selective. All relevant information should be included.

  2. As report writers we are under a duty to be fair to all concerned. So for example, we should let people 'speak for themselves' even if we personally consider that their account is mistaken, or worse.

  3. By demonstrating balance, you are not detracting from the force of your argument. On the contrary, you are demonstrating your professionalism and authority, and making the criticisms and concerns you raise all the more compelling.

In the same way, it is important that the language we use is professional and cannot be read as containing a personal or moral judgement about people or their behaviour. As an example, consider the following extract from a report:

Example of bad writing

Despite Mr Z's protests, I managed to see the kitchen. It was disgusting. I could not believe anyone prepared food there.

This may be perfectly understandable as a first reaction on the worker's part. The problem is that words like 'disgusting' are subjective and contain no 'hard' information. A detailed description of (in this case) unhygienic conditions will be much more helpful for the conference if it confines itself to factual observations about what was found. Striving to be as objective as possible is also likely to make the account more authoritative and professional.

We would like to conclude this chapter with comment from Roger Vickers:

Expert's experience and comment

Case conference reports vary in quality but are not usually as bad as strategy meeting reports. However, they often indicate that persons who should not be present for the whole of a meeting remain and amazingly are sometimes allowed to vote on whether or not abuse took place. I have seen family members voting on this (what about trying to help future civil claims) and also representatives of companies have voted on whether institutional abuse has taken place!

When a case conference deems that on the balance of probability abuse has taken place, this can have serious consequences for any supposed perpetrator. This person can be moved from a particular role, suspended from duty or even dismissed. The decision about whether or not abuse has taken place should be taken by professionals and based on evidence and not influenced by anyone with a possible vested interest.

I also think the more serious the allegation and possible consequences, the conference should be careful that it does not go on a 51–49 per cent balance, but [should aim] to be much more sure and get further up towards a 75–25 per cent level.

Clearly family members, involved organisations and perpetrators should be present for a part of the meeting and provide views. They should then leave while the conference comes to a professional decision based on evidence. The evidence relied on should be recorded and a note made as to why this is being given more weight than other evidence and what may have been said by those now excluded.

I am very surprised that case conference chairs have not been legally challenged in the civil courts when allowing case conferences to come to a conclusion having not followed good practice or natural justice.

If the Chair keeps the conference tight and is given time to plan it properly it should be to the point and relatively short, something like:

• description of events (seek agreement)

- what do these disclose in terms of practice (good, poor or indifferent)?
- is the practice sufficiently poor to amount to some sort of abuse?
- what is the evidence for this?
- what do alleged perpetrators have to say?
- what do organisations have to say?
- what do family members/legal representatives have to say?
- ask all but professionals to leave
- accurately minute discussion
- come to conclusion
- ask those excluded to return
- announce decision and why it is reached
- ask for short comments.
- close.

If the approach to strategy meetings and case conferences is seen to be independent and fair then the process is likely to be better supported, leading to more willingness to raise alerts in the knowledge that any repercussions for individuals/organisations will be based on a proper process and firm evidence. This will improve the safety of all vulnerable adults.

Roger Vickers

Suggested reading

We suggest that a worker should read their local Safeguarding Adults Policy and Procedure; become familiar with the procedures but also the written documentation which is required.

Chapter 8

Risk Assessment and Developing Safeguarding Plans

All workers mention the work 'risk' at some point in the course of their daily work. The public at large is very conscious of risk in relation to health and safety issues and some people think we are now 'over cautious' in the way we deal with risk. Risk assessment and risk management are an integral part of safeguarding adults work. Unfortunately training on adult abuse does not often cover in enough depth *how* to assess risk when dealing with a suspicion or allegation about abuse or how the risk assessment fits into the investigation process. Pritchard has written extensively on risk assessment and developed particular tools for safeguarding adults work (Pritchard 2007; 2008). The aim of this chapter is to summarise that work in relation to how risk assessments should be written before developing a safeguarding plan.[1] It is not an objective to discuss the practices of how alerts should be responded to or how investigations should be conducted. Ideally any safeguarding adults policy should have a risk assessment tool within it so that any worker can use the tool – even before making an alert.

It is important that workers understand and use the correct terminology; there is a tendency to interchange words whilst talking about risk. When organisations are working in partnership they should all be using the same terminology so that they understand each other and are working towards the same end. Unfortunately, because so many risk tools exist for different purposes within organisations, the end result is often confusion for workers. So let us be clear about how risk assessment fits into safeguarding adults work. This book is about recording so must give a clear message that risk should not just be talked about in strategy

---

1   The term 'safeguarding plan' will be adopted in the chapter, but relates to what some workers still refer to as a 'protection plan'. The terms are synonymous.

meetings and case conferences, risk assessments must be produced in a written format.

Risk assessment before alerting

Sometimes thinking about risk and the possibility of harm to the victim of abuse can focus a worker on making a better alert. Many workers are 'scared of getting it wrong' and may harbour their fears that a service user is being abused for quite some time before reporting to their line manager. When dwelling on something and what action to take it is often helpful to try to make a list of concerns but also to verbalise thoughts and feelings. Whilst reflecting, a worker can make a list of their concerns which will help them verbalise in a more concise way when they go to their manager.

It often happens that whilst talking to a manager things become clearer. It is during such discussions that a very basic risk assessment can be done; the word 'basic' is used deliberately because information available can be scant at this stage. Nevertheless, if these concerns are going to be passed on as a formal alert it can be useful to include a risk assessment with any other documentation which is going to be sent through to adult social care. All workers should check whether a risk tool is included in their local safeguarding adults policy; if not, then a worker should write a separate risk assessment and attach it to any form or report which has been completed to make the alert. This does not have to be an in-depth risk assessment. A worker can adopt the simple headings which are in the risk tool presented later in this chapter.

Risk assessment during a strategy meeting

Most policies state that information should be gathered before a strategy meeting is convened. The amount of information available will differ from case to case. Nevertheless, risk assessment must be formally discussed during the course of this meeting. If it is a formal sit-down meeting then risk assessment will be a recurring theme throughout the discussion, but it should also be an agenda item where the grading of risk can be formally agreed. However, in some cases there is a need for a speedy response because of the nature of the alert and the strategy meeting may take place on the telephone. For example a manager of a team might have telephone discussions with personnel in other agencies, such as the police, or Care Quality Commission. As was discussed in Chapter 7, the manager should be taking notes as these discussions occur (i.e. keeping contemporaneous notes); in addition it is imperative that the manager must introduce the subject of risk assessment during the discussions. If a risk tool is available in the local safeguarding adults policy, the manager should use that as a focus for the discussions which take place.

Whether the strategy meeting is conducted on the telephone or as a formal meeting a risk assessment must be undertaken and when required an interim safeguarding plan should be developed. The objective of such a plan is to ensure that the alleged victim of abuse can be kept safe whilst an investigation takes place. It is important to remind ourselves at this point that some alleged abusers will be a vulnerable adult themselves, and an interim safeguarding plan may need to be developed for that person.

Whatever type of strategy meeting takes place, it is the responsibility of the chairperson to ensure that the risk assessment and any interim safeguarding plan are written up properly and circulated with the minutes of the meeting.

Risk assessment during a case conference

Investigating officers who undertake an abuse investigation have a responsibility to assess the risk of significant harm and address this in their report to the case conference. Whilst they are interviewing the alleged victim and other people with a view to gathering evidence, they are risk assessing. The role of the investigating officers in gathering evidence is two-fold: (i) to prove whether abuse has been substantiated or not; and (ii) to predict whether the alleged victim is likely to experience significant harm in the future. If it is concluded that the victim is likely to be harmed, then a safeguarding plan has to be produced in order to demonstrate and evidence in writing how organisations are going to work together in order to minimise the likelihood of harm occurring in the future. The plan should then be monitored and reviewed through convening review case conferences. Once a safeguarding plan has been developed the risk management process is in place.

It just needs to be reiterated that a risk assessment will focus on the victim of abuse. However, where the alleged abuser is also a vulnerable adult then a separate risk assessment might be undertaken for that individual and presented to a case conference convened specifically for the alleged abuser because of their difficulties. Any safeguarding plan for an abuser would follow the same risk management process, namely, through review case conferences.

Significant harm

Before going on to consider how the risk assessment should be written, it is necessary to discuss why the term 'significant harm' is important. The term has been used in child protection work for many years and when *No Secrets* was introduced in 2000, Section 2.18 stated:

> 'harm' should be taken to include…not only ill treatment (including sexual abuse and forms of ill treatment which are not physical), but also the impairment of, or an avoidable deterioration in, physical or mental health; and the impairment of physical, intellectual, emotional, social or behavioural development. (DH 2000, p.12)

In any risk assessment it is necessary to try to predict how likely it is that a person may be harmed if they take risk, or are exposed to risk by others. In safeguarding adults work it is necessary to use this definition of harm when undertaking risk assessment. However, it must be said that this definition does not transfer easily to those adults who have cognitive or other communication problems as it is often very difficult to measure how significant the harm has been for that individual, because they cannot tell a worker and it is impossible to measure it in any other way.

Writing a risk assessment

The art of writing good risk assessments is to follow some very simple rules which are outlined below.

BEST PRACTICE POINTS

- Write short sentences which are clear and to the point.
- Do not use holistic, generic terms which are too broad and meaningless.
- Be specific.
- Expand and give more detail when explanation is really needed (to explain why something is a hazard or danger – see below).
- Use correct terminology, as misunderstandings can have serious consequences.
- State if the victim/abuser lacks capacity in relation to a specific issue.
- Include the views, wishes and feelings of the victim (or abuser if a separate risk assessment is being undertaken for that person).
- Include opinions of others.

Using the correct terminology when writing

In order to explain more about how to write a risk assessment we shall talk through the terminology and ask the reader to refer to the risk tool presented in the handout that follows. This tool was developed to be utilised specifically when working with adult abuse (Pritchard 2007; 2008).

Risk-taking action

In day-to-day risk assessment a worker should ask: 'What does the service user want to do?' This is still a valid question when dealing with an abuse case but a worker has to be mindful that a victim of abuse may be in a situation where they are taking (or being exposed to) risks but they have no choice about it, that is, they are being controlled by the abuser and forced into a situation.

Examples of risk-taking actions

- To continue to live in the abusive situation.

- To sign ownership of the house over to a family member.

- To drink to excess.

- To stay in bed all day.

- To refuse to accept any services.

- To refuse to make a statement to the police.

- To suddenly decline to let the regular home care workers into the house.

Handout: Risk assessment tool

Name of service user			ID Code	

Alleged/suspected/proven categories of abuse:

Name of worker(s) and job title completing the risk tool:

1 | **RISK-TAKING ACTION (S)** | ⓘ *What does the service user want to do?*

2 | **BENEFITS** | ⓘ *Why does the service user want to take the risk? What will s/he get out of it?*

3 | **HAZARDS** | ⓘ *Can be anything, e.g. person, behaviour, situation which stops the benefit or causes the danger.*

4 DANGERS

1

2

3

4

5

6

7

8

9

10

11

12

5 PREDICTION/LIKELIHOOD

ⓘ Key question: How likely
is the danger will occur?

Prediction Scale

VERY LIKELY	QUITE LIKELY	NOT VERY LIKELY	NOT AT ALL LIKELY

	DANGER	EVIDENCE	PRESENTED BY	PREDICTION
1				
2				
3				
4				
5				
6				

Prediction Scale

VERY LIKELY	QUITE LIKELY	NOT VERY LIKELY	NOT AT ALL LIKELY

DANGER	EVIDENCE	PRESENTED BY	PREDICTION
7			
8			
9			
10			
11			
12			

6 <u>CONFLICT BOX</u>

ⓘ *To be used when a person disagrees with a decision or grading.*

<u>NAME OF PERSON</u>

<u>EXPLAIN WHAT S/HE DISAGREES WITH</u>

7 | DEVELOPMENT OF PROTECTION PLAN

ⓘ *Detail needed about objectives, agencies, personnel, roles, responsibilities, tasks, contact, method of working, monitoring tools, written records.*

8 GRADING OF CASE

LOW ☐   MODERATE ☐   HIGH ☐

9 DATE FOR REVIEW

Date [   ]   Time [   ]

10 SIGNATURES

NAME	JOB TITLE/ RELATIONSHIP	SIGNATURE	DATE
	Service User		
	Worker		
	Manager		

Benefit

This is a term which is often missing from a risk assessment form. A benefit is the positive outcome that a person wants to achieve through taking the risk. It is important to discuss with the person why they want to take the risk or in the case of a victim of abuse asking them to explain the reasons for staying with the abuser. Writing a proper social history and including it in this section of a risk assessment can give a clear insight into the situation. It can also be helpful to use actual quotes from victims in order express their views and feelings plainly.

Examples of benefits

- maintaining a relationship with the abuser who is loved dearly ('He's my son. He does not mean to hurt me. It's not his fault' – mother being physically and financially abused)

- having visitors

- not being lonely

- living in a familiar situation, that is, with no change ('better the devil you know' – victim of domestic violence)

- following religious or spiritual beliefs

- being accepted within a culture

- not being different

- does not upset the abuser.

Hazard

In simple terms a hazard can stop a person getting the benefit they want to achieve, or it can directly cause a danger. A hazard can be absolutely anything, for example, person, object, medical condition, disability, personality trait, physical or mental health problem, environment, or situation. It is important to think about what influences exist in a person's life which affect their risk-taking. However, it is important not to just focus on the victim; it can be helpful for a worker to think about the actions, behaviours, or characteristics of the abuser which may constitute some of the hazards which exist.

Workers can often struggle to differentiate between a hazard and a danger. Sometimes a certain 'thing' could be either; typical examples are self-harm, depression, anxiety. This is why it is important to first of all be clear about what the risk-taking action is exactly. In order to focus a worker on understanding the hazards in a case, it is useful to ask the following questions:

KEY QUESTIONS

- What is stopping the victim getting the benefit?
- Are there particular problems, difficulties, conditions?
- What is actually causing the dangers?
- What does the abuser do to the victim?
- What is the abuser like? (personality, behaviour traits).
- Is there any related past history? (of violence, offending, such as assault, theft).

Examples of hazards

- lack of insight
- lack of confidence
- low self-esteem
- too trusting
- desperate for affection
- being lonely
- love
- guilt

- violent behaviour
- shouting
- swearing
- threatening behaviour
- need for money
- gambling
- debts
- addiction/misuse – alcohol, drugs.

Danger

A danger is the worst feared outcome, that is, the negative outcomes. One of the main tasks in risk assessment is to predict what those negative outcomes might be and how likely they are to happen. When thinking about abuse situations it is important to first link the dangers to the categories of abuse as stated in *No Secrets*, that is:

- physical

- sexual

- emotional/psychological

- financial/material

- neglect/act of omission

- discriminatory.

(DH 2000, p.9)

After highlighting the categories of abuse which may happen in the future, other dangers can then be listed and explained.

Examples of dangers

- injuries

- loss of sight

- self-harm

- low self-worth

- suicide

- electricity and gas disconnections

- eviction/homelessness

- debt.

Good risk assessments are about giving detail, being explicit and not using global terms that do not tell us anything. For example, writing 'personal hygiene' as a hazard is terribly vague but the following list of hazards tells us more:

- Has refused to wash or bath for the past six weeks.

- Wears the same clothes day and night.

- Uses newspaper for toilet paper.

Another example: 'confusion' is the global term, but more helpful are the hazards stated as:

- Sally has been diagnosed as being in the early stages of Alzheimer's disease, which causes her to have some confusion at certain times of the day.

- She believes that Roger Green, another resident, is her husband.

- She repeatedly asks Roger to come into her bed at night.

The above examples are meant to illustrate some detail. It is important for a worker to think about how they will present hazards and dangers both in content and layout.

> **BEST PRACTICE POINTS**
> - State the hazard or danger briefly, in three or four words or a very short sentence.
> - Underneath write a fuller explanation evidencing why something is a hazard or what the danger would entail.

Exercise 8.1 will help workers to think in terms of hazards and dangers. Once this exercise has been undertaken on a training course or during supervision, workers should be encouraged to continue to think about the risks they take in their personal lives once they are away from work. This can be done by agreeing to allocate a half an hour period per day when a worker is not at work to assess themselves when doing the most simplest of tasks. This is encouraging a worker to practise thinking in terms of of hazards and dangers but also bringing a bit of light relief to a serious subject as the following example shows.

EXERCISE 8.1

WRITING ABOUT HAZARDS AND DANGERS

OBJECTIVE

For workers to think about hazards and dangers a victim of abuse might experience.

To write in plain language and avoid global terms and jargon.

PARTICIPANTS

Individual or group work.

EQUIPMENT

Paper and pens.

TIME

15 minutes.

TASK

1. Think about adults who have been abused or cases where abuse has been suspected.

2. Make a list of the hazards from all the adult abuse cases you have thought about. Complete this before going onto Task 3.

3. Make a list of the dangers from the adults abuse cases you have considered.

4. Write in the same way as you would on a real risk assessment.

Case example: Personal risk-taking

Risk-taking action: To put on the kettle (after coming home from the pub on a Friday night).

Benefits: To enjoy a cup of coffee after drinking some wine after a very hard week at work.

Hazards: Having drunk more wine than planned.
Feeling a bit tipsy.
Taken out contact lenses so cannot see very well.
Shaking hands.
Boiling water.

Dangers: Pour water onto hand rather than into mug.
Burn on hand.

Evidence and predicting likelihood

The key tasks in risk assessment are to predict the:

- positive outcomes (benefits) and negative outcomes (dangers) of the risk-taking action

- likelihood of the dangers occurring.

Before being able to make any predictions in regard to likelihood, evidence has to be presented. This is one of the main reasons for producing written reports for safeguarding adults meetings. Reports need to be written in a way that presents the evidence needed for a risk assessment; it makes the task less onerous in the meeting because most of the work has already been done. Evidence is based on:

- current circumstances

- environment

- past behaviours/incidents

- frequency of incidents

- duration of incidents

- vulnerability of the victim

- dangerousness of the abuser.

Risk of harm to whom and what?

Workers must think about harm in relation to public protection. It is not just about assessing risk of harm to the victim in an abuse case, workers have to think about risk of harm to the general public (this could include workers, and/or other service users) and property. Therefore, anyone contributing to a risk assessment should understand the following terms and be thinking about them during the process of assessing risk:

- risk assessment

- risk management

- significant harm

- likelihood/probability

- public protection

- dangerousness.

Writing and completing the risk tool (pp.148–154)

The first four sections of the risk tool (i.e. risk-taking action, benefits, hazards and dangers) should be completed before a strategy meeting or a case conference; then the chairperson at those meetings should lead the participants through the rest of the tool in order to complete the risk assessment. It is not the purpose of this chapter to discuss this process but what must be said is that it is the chairperson's responsibility to ensure that a consensus of opinion is reached regarding the likelihood of each danger occurring. The gradings are:

- very likely

- quite likely

- not very likely

- not at all likely.

A grading must be entered on the tool in Section 5 for each danger listed. If reports have been written it is possible for the chairperson to cross-reference to these reports in the column entitled 'evidence'. If someone refuses to go with the consensus of opinion, then the reasons for the refusal/disagreement must be entered in the conflict box (Section 6).

Whereas Section 5 is looking specifically at each danger which has been predicted, Section 7 on the tool is focusing on the situation as a whole, that is, whether the victim is likely to experience 'significant harm' in the future before the [interim] safeguarding plan is put in place. The risk has to be graded low, medium or high. Again if there is any dissent amongst people contributing to the assessment this would be written down in the conflict box. It is critical to have an overall grading of the case because the date for review will be set depending on the level of risk of significant harm which has been predicted. When review case conferences are convened it is necessary to measure whether the degree of risk has increased, decreased or remained the same.

The minutes of any meeting are a record of what has been said and agreed. However, best practice is for people to sign a document to say they agree with something. Hence, the reason for having Section 10 of the risk tool. This should be passed round the table so that participants (including the service user) of a meeting sign up to the risk assessment and safeguarding plan; this promotes working in partnership but also ensures joint accountability.

BEST PRACTICE POINTS

- Risk assessment involves writing down people's views and opinions, that is, it is a record which can be referred back to when necessary.
- Consensus of opinion must be reached regarding the likelihood of each danger occurring.
- Consensus of opinion must be reached regarding the likelihood of significant harm occurring, namely, an overall grading of the case.
- Disagreements must be recorded in the conflict box.
- Any refusal to agree with the content of the safeguarding plan must be recorded in the conflict box.
- Everyone who participated in the risk assessment should put their signature on the form (this should include the service user or their IMCA/advocate).

The best way to get better at writing risk assessments is to get some practice. The following exercise can be used in a training session or a manager could give one case study to a worker and ask them to complete the risk assessment tool.

EXERCISE 8.2

WRITING ABOUT RISKS, HAZARDS AND DANGERS

OBJECTIVE

To help participants understand the terms used in risk assessment and to develop writing to fully explain a risk, hazard and danger.

PARTICIPANTS

Small groups in a training session or for an individual worker.

EQUIPMENT

Flipchart paper and pens.
Copies of Handout 8.2.

TIME

45 minutes.

TASK

1. Each group/worker will be asked to work on just one scenario from the cases listed on Handout 8.2.

2. The group/worker will be asked to answer the following questions:

   a. What are the risk-taking action(s)?

   b. What are the hazards?

   c. What are the dangers?

   d. At this moment in time how would you grade the risk of significant harm – low, moderate or high? This grading should NOT be written down, but agreed verbally.

3. Participants will be asked to have a full discussion before writing down their answers. The answers should be written down in the same way that a risk assessment would be presented, i.e. full sentences, including good detail and explanation.

FEEDBACK

1. In a training session one scenario will be taken at a time. The group will feed back from their flipchart sheets. They will not share their grading of risk of significant harm at this point.

2. Other groups will comment on what has been presented. After a full discussion the other groups will offer their opinion regarding the grading of risk of significant harm. The group who has worked on the scenario will then share what their grading was; if there are any disagreements a full discussion should ensue.

Handout for Exercise 8.2

Abraham, who is slightly confused, has been attending the day centre for six months now and has settled in well. However, over the past two weeks he has said to two members of staff that he does not like the new day care worker, Tina. Today he breaks down and cries; he says that Tina has no patience, is very bad tempered and has shouted at him and other service users on several occasions. He also said that he has seen her slap another service user who is in the advanced stages of Alzheimer's disease.

Colette has moderate learning disabilities and is living independently with the help of a support worker. She likes to be with people rather than being on her own, so goes out as much as she can and likes to make new friends. She is very trusting and does not ever think badly of people. Colette has got into the routine of going out every other night to the local pub, where she has met two men Eamon and Andrew; it is known that both men have served prison sentences for sexual offences in relation to children. Colette likes the men because they buy her alcoholic drinks; however in recent weeks she has not been able to remember what has happened between Friday night and Sunday night. She tells her support worker, 'it's all missing in my head.'

Victoria has red marks and bruises on her face which are seen by the home care worker when she visits today. Simon, Victoria's son who is the primary carer, discloses that he lost his temper last night and hit his mother. Simon says that this is not the first time he has done this and says it is because he is finding it very hard to cope with her since she developed dementia.

Kyle is 21 years old and recently been diagnosed as having schizophrenia. He was taken into care at the age of 12 and lived in several children's homes and with foster families. He has been sexually abused by various people through his childhood. He has a very low opinion of himself and believes that everything is his fault, 'because that's what everyone has always told me.' He has no family and is very lonely. He recently joined a local support group run by a religious organisation for adults who have been abused in childhood. The leaders of the group have told members that they are to blame for their abuse and they must forgive their abuser. As penance, they are encouraged to give money to the organisation.

Polly, who has dementia, is cared for by her younger sister Louise, aged 55, who gave up her full-time job in a hotel to care for her sister. Recently Louise was asked to return to work on reception a few nights a week, which she was eager to do. When she goes out to work Louise locks Polly in her bedroom. She does not have access to food, drink or the toilet. Polly screams and bangs on the door when Louise leaves. Each time she returns Louise finds that Polly has damaged things in the room and she has often hurt herself in the process.

The previous exercise contained short case scenarios. What follows is a more in-depth case study which can be used in conjunction with the risk tool. A worker can be asked to complete the risk tool in anticipation that Errol might go to live in a communal setting where other vulnerable people may be resident or visiting the establishment.

Case study: Errol (age 79)

Errol is an African-Caribbean man who is about to be released from prison. He has been inside for 15 years having murdered a young prostitute. He has had no letters, visits or telephone contact with any members of his family since being imprisoned.

Errol has had diabetes throughout his adulthood, but since being in prison he has developed a lot of other health problems. He has angina and his mobility is very poor. A year ago he started to become confused. The medical officer thinks he 'probably has a bit of dementia but he can function well enough' and as his release date drew near suggested, 'The assessment can be done properly on the outside.'

The prison service has done a risk assessment regarding the likelihood of Errol re-offending; he is thought to be a low risk. He will be released back into the community on licence and a probation officer will be monitoring him. In preparation for his release, adult social care have been contacted and also the Alzheimer's Society with a view to offering Errol some support. It is thought that he may benefit from contact with other older people in the local community, but he will also need help readjusting to the changes in society.

However, there are concerns because of his past history. Prior to his sentencing for murder, Errol had committed other violent offences – always towards women. Prison officers say that he is a 'very bitter man who lashes out verbally and physically.' He has been attacked on a number of occasions by other inmates. Errol is going to live in a probation hostel temporarily on release; but it has been suggested that he be assessed for housing in sheltered accommodation.

Safeguarding plans

When undertaking risk assessments in day-to-day work, workers will develop care plans. In safeguarding adults work, risk assessment is an ongoing process which is formalised in strategy meetings and case conferences. It has been mentioned already that interim or full safeguarding plans may be developed. Over the years the term protection plan has been used; a safeguarding plan has the same objective, that is, to show how an adult can be protected from harm.

> **BEST PRACTICE POINT**
>
> - A safeguarding plan should demonstrate clearly and in detail how agencies, workers and other individuals are going to try to minimise the risk of harm occurring.

The reality is that in many cases a victim may choose to stay in an abusive situation and also refuse help. The ultimate aim for workers will be to monitor those situations, but unlike in safeguarding children workers do not automatically have the right of entry to do so. Therefore it is important to strive to work towards engaging the adult in developing any safeguarding plan.

> **BEST PRACTICE POINT**
>
> - A safeguarding plan is something you develop *with* the adult;[2] it is not something which can be imposed upon them.

If a safeguarding plan is to be developed, then it should be written in a comprehensive way. We can learn from how child protection has progressed over the years and how protection plans for children were developed by establishing a core group of people. The principles regarding promoting safety and working together are the same whether working with children or adults:

> **5.82** The initial child protection conference brings together family members, the child who is the subject of the conference (where

---

2   Remembering that a plan can be developed for a victim or an abuser if the latter is a vulnerable adult.

appropriate) and those professionals most involved with the child and family, following section 47 enquiries. Its purpose is:

- to bring together and analyse, in an inter-agency setting, the information which has been obtained about the child's developmental needs and the parents' or carers' capacity to respond to these needs to ensure the child's safety and promote the child's health and development, within the context of their wider family and environment;

- to consider the evidence presented to the conference and taking into account the child's present situation and information about his or her family history and present and past family functioning, make judgements about the likelihood of the child suffering significant harm in future and decide whether the child is continuing to, or is likely to, suffer significant harm; and

- to decide what future action is required in order to safeguard and promote the welfare of the child, including the child becoming the subject of a child protection plan, what the planned developmental outcomes are for the child and how best to intervene to achieve these.

(HM Government 2010, p.161)

Unfortunately, in safeguarding adults work sometimes the safeguarding plan is not written in enough detail; for example it is written as a series of bullet points at the end of minutes from a strategy meeting or case conference. It is important to make the point which has been a central theme throughout this book that organisations and workers have to evidence what they do; this is achieved by recording in detail decisions and actions and the reasons behind them. The minutes of safeguarding adults meetings should include this detail regarding decision-making, but the objective in writing a safeguarding plan is to show:

- details regarding the victim and abuser
- which categories of abuse are suspected or have been proven
- the main objectives of the plan
- who is going to be involved
- how the objectives are going to be achieved

- timescales for work
- date for review.

This is discussed further below. The decisions and recommendations from the strategy meeting/case conferences should form the skeleton of any safeguarding plan. People who are going to be involved in the plan will form a core group and meet with the adult in order to write the plan in detail.

What should be included in a safeguarding plan

Every safeguarding plan is going to vary because circumstances will be different for each individual. For example, a victim may:

- choose to remain in an abusive situation, but agree to workers monitoring them
- have moved to a place a safety whilst the investigation takes place
- have left an abusive situation permanently, but need practical help and emotional support for the future
- continue to deny that abuse is occurring
- not have the capacity to disclose about abuse.

The safeguarding plan should include several distinct sections; some of which need to be concise and others will need to include finite detail.

Details of the victim and abuser

At the top of any safeguarding plan, basic details regarding the [alleged] victim and [alleged] abuser should be stated together with the categories of abuse which have been alleged, suspected, disclosed, proven.

Objective

This section should be short and to the point. It is helpful to include information about:

- the main objectives of the plan, namely, the decisions and recommendations from the strategy meeting/case conference
- which categories of abuse have been alleged, substantiated or are still suspected (depending on which stage of the process has been reached).

Example of bad writing

Aim of the plan: to monitor Mrs Hammond who is being abused by her son. Will review as agreed in case conference.

What would have been better

It has been substantiated that Mrs Hammond is being financially abused on a regular basis by her son, Sean, who lives in the same household and has a gambling problem. Mrs Hammond has also experienced physical abuse on two occasions. Mrs Hammond acknowledges what is happening and readily talks about Sean stealing from her, but does not want any action taken against her son. However, she has said that she would welcome ongoing support and the opportunity to talk about the problems which exist. It was agreed at the case conference that Gayle Best, social worker, will offer support (see below for detail) for two months and then a review case conference will be convened on 14 December 2010.

Core group of people involved

It is imperative to give details of people who are going to be involved in a safeguarding plan. The reason for this is explained by a lawyer:

Expert's experience and comment

Whether we are talking child abuse or adult abuse the principle for writing good protection plans is the same – detail. I should be able to pick up a plan and not have to look at anything else on the file. It should tell me exactly how a person is being protected. If I want to contact one of the core group I shouldn't have to spend time wading through a file; it should all be on the protection plan.

Lawyer

So the following contact details should be listed for each person involved in the plan:

- name
- job title and organisation or relationship to the person (e.g. family member; friend; neighbour)

- postal address

- e-mail address

- telephone number

- fax number

- mobile number.

It is good to have a nominated *keyworker* for a safeguarding plan, whose main responsibility is to co-ordinate the plan. If a problem arises with the plan, for example, something is not working or someone is not doing what they agreed at the meeting, then this should be reported back to the keyworker. This person will normally be someone like a social worker, community psychiatric nurse, nurse on a learning disability team. In addition it is possible to have a named *primary worker*, that is, someone who has most face-to-face contact with the victim/abuser. The core group of people are dealing with the safeguarding issues explicitly and therefore could be a wide range of people: professional, worker, family member, friend, neighbour, volunteer, advocate.

Responsibilities and tasks

This is the really important part of the safeguarding plan where exact detail is given about *who* is going to *what* and *when*. This is reminiscent of what was discussed about basic recording skills in Chapter 4. The following needs to be included regarding each person who has a role in the plan:

- name, job title or relationship with victim/abuser

- objectives – what he or she is trying to achieve

- responsibilities and tasks

- methods to be used

- contact – frequency and duration

- venue for contact.

Examples of bad writing

1. Social worker will visit Mrs Hammond regularly.

2. Telephone support also to be offered.

What would have been better

- Gayle Best, social worker, will visit Mrs Hammond once a week until the review case conference is convened. Mrs Hammond would prefer Gayle to visit in the afternoon when Sean is in the betting shop; she does not mind which day of the week.

- Mrs Hammond is keen to have telephone contact with Gayle in between visits. Gayle will ring Mrs Hammond each Friday afternoon to review how the week has been and to arrange an appointment for the following week. In addition, Mrs Hammond knows she can ring Gayle if she is feeling frightened or just needs to talk. Mrs Hammond has also been given the name of Gayle's manager and telephone number for when Gayle is on leave (week commencing 8 November 2010).

- Gayle will visit for one hour every week to give Mrs Hammond the opportunity to talk about Sean and the relationship she has with him. Mrs Hammond is aware that this is the opportunity to talk about her feelings and fears. Gayle will also work on personal safety issues and assertiveness skills.

- Mrs Hammond has asked Gayle to bring her some information about the local Gamblers Anonymous meetings and support for family members.

- Gayle has made it clear to Mrs Hammond that she will have to report any further instances of violence should they occur in the future.

Monitoring

Each person who is involved in a safeguarding plan should have stated in the strategy meeting/case conference how they are going to monitor the work undertaken. The word 'monitor' can be a bit of a cliché. If the following questions are asked and answered a better safeguarding plan will be written:

KEY QUESTIONS

- What is being monitored?
- Will particular tools or protocols be used? (e.g. to monitor changes in behaviour, mood, injuries).
- What records will be kept?
- Where will the records be stored?
- How will the information be presented at the review case conference?

Date for review

Whether a case conference is an initial or review one, a date for review should be set for the future if a safeguarding plan is going to be implemented. The date for review should be linked to the grading of risk, namely, whether it is a low, moderate or high-risk case. The date which has been set for review should be written on the safeguarding plan.

Who should have the plan

When a plan has been agreed in a strategy meeting or case conference, then it should be written up formally as described above and circulated with the minutes of the meeting. If the vulnerable adult has not been present at the meeting, they must not be forgotten (which they often are!) – she or he should have a copy. If the person lacks capacity and would not understand the plan then their advocate should have a copy and deal with this in the best possible way.

Reviewing the plan

Once a safeguarding plan has been developed and implemented then the stage of risk management has been reached. Risk management is an ongoing process and involves reviewing a plan at regular intervals – depending on the grading of risk. Geraldine Monaghan describes what has been a central theme through this book – the need for preparation, analysis and detail:

Expert's experience and comment

If the plan stated we needed to do X and Y by May and we did not do it by September then in addition to 'Why not?' the question should be 'What do we need to do now?' We need succinct assessment summary. Key considerations are: what did we set out to do; how did we intend to do it; was it done or not; if not, why not; what do we need to do now; do we need to do anything else? Key questions are: how, what, why and when.

Geraldine Monaghan

Conclusion

This chapter has been looking at the importance of risk assessment in safeguarding adults work and emphasising how it is important that the assessment and management of risk needs to be written down clearly by developing a detailed safeguarding plan. Workers may sigh at the thought of having to produce more paperwork, but risk assessment should not just be a verbal exercise.

Suggested reading

Brearley, C.P. (1982) *Risk and Ageing.* London: Routledge and Kegan Paul.

Brearley, C.P. (1982) *Risk in Social Work.* London: Routledge and Kegan Paul.

HM Government (2010) *Working Together to Safeguard Children.* London: The Stationery Office. Particularly paragraphs 5.97–106 on developing protection plans.

Kemshall, H. and Pritchard, J. (eds) (1996) *Good Practice in Risk Assessment and Risk Management,* Volume 1. London: Jessica Kingsley Publishers.

Kemshall, H. and Pritchard, J. (eds) (1997) *Good Practice in Risk Assessment and Risk Management 2: Protection, Rights and Responsibilities.* London: Jessica Kingsley Publishers.

Pritchard, J. (2007) 'Risk assessment and developing protection plans.' In J. Pritchard *Working with Adult Abuse: A Training Manual for People Working with Vulnerable Adults.* London: Jessica Kingsley Publishers.

Pritchard, J. (2008) 'Doing risk assessment properly in adult protection work.' In J. Pritchard (ed.) *Good Practice in Safeguarding Adults: Working Effectively in Adult Protection.* London: Jessica Kingsley Publishers.

Chapter 9

Minute-Taking in Safeguarding Adults Meetings

Minute-taking in safeguarding adults work is rarely undertaken in the same way as at child protection meetings and hence the standards are often inadequate. In some areas of the country safeguarding adults units or teams have had designated minute-takers for a long time; in other areas managers still struggle to find someone to take the minutes, so end up taking them themselves or asking a participant to do so at the beginning of the meeting. This is not acceptable when the safeguarding of adults should be just as important as the safeguarding of children and therefore the standards we strive for in working with adults should be equal to those in child care. So there are still very few areas which have minute-takers trained specifically for safeguarding adults meetings. This chapter will explain how minutes should be taken and throughout there will be clear explanation regarding why this is important for evidential purposes.

What is a safeguarding adults meeting?

We are using the term safeguarding adults meeting because we are aware that within different areas of the UK terminology can vary. It is important that minutes of a meeting state clearly what type of meeting has taken place. A comment which is heard frequently on abuse training courses is, 'I was asked to attend a meeting, but I don't know what sort of meeting it was.' The majority of safeguarding adults policies refer to strategy meetings and case conferences. However, others have a: planning meeting; risk planning meeting; protection plan meeting.

Workers often talk verbally about having a 'professionals meeting' (many of which seem to be convened without the service user knowing, which begs the question whether their human rights are being contravened). Any meetings convened regarding a case where there are concerns about abuse must be called by their title as stated in the local policy and procedures. For the purpose of this chapter we are going to refer to any meeting called under a safeguarding policy and procedure a *safeguarding adults meeting*.

Different types of minute-taking

It is necessary to go back to where we were at the very beginning of this book and focus on *purpose*. Nowadays there is a wide range of publications on how to take minutes and in the corporate world there are many training organisations offering courses to train administrative staff how to take minutes. There is a great emphasis on brevity. However, the minutes which need to be taken in safeguarding adults meetings need to be different from the type of minutes taken in a business meeting. It is necessary to remind ourselves at this point that minutes from such meetings can be used as evidence. The notes a minute-taker has written during a meeting can be considered as contemporaneous notes and therefore they should be kept. The minutes which are to be circulated to participants should be cut down to form a shorter version.

Teamwork: relationship between the chairperson and minute-taker

In order to take good minutes in a meeting, the chairperson and minute-taker need to work as a team. Once again the word *communication* comes into play. The chairperson and minute-taker must communicate before, during and after a meeting. Best practice would suggest that a manager and an administrative person should regularly work together in safeguarding meetings so they get to know each other well which enables them to communicate effectively in different ways – using discussion, listening skills, body language (especially eye contact). Both individuals need to get to know how the other one works. All chairpersons have their own styles; minute-takers need to understand this and how it might affect their way of working. A minute-taker should never be intimidated or scared to ask for help. The responsibilities of a chairperson to a minute-taker are listed below.

BEST PRACTICE POINTS

A chairperson should:

- explain what they expect from the minute-taker
- give advice and guidance
- listen to the minute-taker
- check notes and draft minutes
- debrief the minute-taker after a meeting
- offer practical and emotional support as required
- see the minute-taker as an equal not as a minion.

When training and developing minute-takers for safeguarding adults work some thought must be given to how minute-takers are going to be asked to do the job, that is, what systems are in place and who they might work alongside. Typical examples are:

- Specialist team/unit have designated minute-takers who will come to know all the chairpersons through doing the job on a daily basis.

- Rota system is in place for team managers to chair safeguarding adults meetings. It is the team manager's responsibility to find a minute-taker; this is usually an administrative person who does minute-taking on top of their normal duties. This means a minute-taker may not come into regular contact with a particular chairperson.

- Buddy system is set up, that is, a team manager who has responsibility for chairing has the same minute-taker for every meeting. This is usually an administrative person on their team or within their specialism.

Before a meeting

Preparing oneself

In order to take good minutes, one of the requirements is that a minute-taker should have ample time to prepare for a meeting. It could be considered an abuse of an administrative person if they are asked to take the minutes of a meeting just 10 minutes before the meeting is due to start. The minute-taker needs time to prepare him or herself and it is always a good idea to make a task list. It is essential to speak to the chairperson about their expectations of the meeting and the minute-taker. The minute-taker needs to ask questions and be honest if they are unsure about anything. It is also important to have a discussion about how important it is for a chairperson to summarise the key points from a discussion at the end of each agenda item or report. This helps the minute-taker greatly when they might have got a bit behind and often highlights if they have missed something. There are a lot of practical tasks which need to be undertaken by the minute-taker, but are not the concern of this particular book which must remain focused on how to take good minutes.

Reading information

It will be important for the minute-taker to read any written information which may help them to have a better understanding of the discussions which may take place in the meeting. For example, if an initial case conference is to be minuted, then it may be helpful to read through the minutes of the strategy meeting which has already taken place. It is important to ask the chairperson if any papers need to be circulated before the meeting takes place (e.g. minutes of previous meetings, reports, etc.) and to read them as background information. The question regarding the limits of confidentiality arises here, so it is useful to state again that any information which is given to a worker is confidential to the organisation which employs that worker; consequently a minute-taker as an employee of that organisation has the right to read documents on a 'need to know' basis. It is imperative that any training course provided for minute-takers does cover the issues surrounding confidentiality and sharing of information.

Equipment and practical things

A minute-taker should always ensure they have the right equipment with them in order to make the taking of minutes easier. The following needs to be considered:

- *Minute-taking book*: There is a lot of controversy about how minutes should be taken. Historically in child protection the original notes have always been taken verbatim in a minute-taking book and then reduced into a shorter version. The minute-taking book has then been archived. The same practices should be followed in safeguarding adults meetings. However, this does not happen on a regular basis due to the lack of time put into this area of work, and also many minute-takers have not had the opportunity to develop the skills to write verbatim.

- *Laptop*: Some minute-takers use a laptop for minute-taking. This raises some concerns. First, this method of minute-taking requires that the minute-taker have the necessary typing speed to keep up with the discussion. All contemporaneous notes should never be altered; using a computer enables such notes to be altered. Steve Kirkpatrick offers some advice on how to ensure that a minute-taker does not alter their original notes:

Expert's experience and comment

I have checked the files on my computer. Right hand mouse click on any file and click on Properties. Then look at the detail tab. Even if files are copied they still retain all the information required by a court. Yes it is open to some computer bods to tamper with it (but this could be proved), but the same could be said of any evidence. All documentary evidence and notes are supported by someone who says, 'I produce this and they were notes that I made on x date. I have not tampered with them. They are the original ones.'

So the PowerPoint presentation I did for a seminar in Nottingham back in 2001 still tells me today [9 years later]:

- It was created on the TVP Loan computer.
- I made 40 revisions!
- I created it at 11.10 on 23/09/2000 (presuming the laptop clock was correct. But again this can be given in evidence).
- I last saved it at 09.27 on 03/12/2001.
- The total editing time was 9 hours and 39 minutes.

It will not let me remove the date created and last saved from it nor from a copy of it. This is the same for my 'Microsoft Works.'

So for minute-takers using a Word or Works document on their laptops I would recommend:

- They name and save the word document before they go into the meeting.
- At the end of the meeting they save their raw copy with typos, incorrect spellings and ungrammatical phrases, etc.

- That this copy is then never edited or deleted. When it is edited a new version saved with a file name such as 'X Edited 08 Jan 2010'.
- The original version is available, if required to a court or tribunal or hearing.

Steve Kirkpatrick

Something which is not always considered but is of paramount importance, is how the victim is going to feel if they are present in the meeting. We raise this point because some victims of abuse struggle with repetitive noise; the sound of the keys on a laptop could irritate such a person. Also it can be generally distracting for other participants.

- *Pens*: a minute-taker should always take notes in black ink (not pencil) and it is a good idea to take a number of spare pens in case a pen runs out or a participant in the meeting needs a pen.

- *Spare paper*: although the minute-taker should be using their book for notes, it is always useful to have spare paper to hand for their own use (see discussion regarding seating plan below) or for participants.

- *Attendance list and signing in sheet*: a common problem for minute-takers is that very often they have to take minutes for a meeting when they have never met any of the participants. Therefore, best practice is that a minute-taker should be told in advance who is going to attend the meeting so that an attendance list can be written and photocopied to aid both the minute-taker, but also participants of the meeting. In addition the minute-taker should always ask participants to put their details on a signing in sheet (see Figure 9.1). This should include their job title, organisation and contact details. This can then be used in conjunction with a seating plan to help with recognising people, and it also helps later when minutes need to be circulated.

- *Place cards*: it also helps the minute-taker if place cards are prepared for the meeting. The names of participants can be printed in a large font on card or white plastic place cards can be purchased in stationery shops. Participants write their names on the cards with ink markers and then they are wiped clean at the end of the meeting.

- *Seating plan*: drawing a seating plan can be a real aid to a minute-taker (see Figure 9.2). It is advisable for a minute-taker to use one of their spare sheets of paper to make a seating plan (if a printed one is not available), which they can keep at the side of them as they are writing in their book. The seating plan can be drawn as people are introducing themselves at the beginning of the meeting.

In the meeting
At the beginning

It is important for the minute-taker to sit next to the chairperson so that they can communicate if necessary; for example if the minute-taker misses something or gets behind she or he must make the chairperson aware of this as soon as possible. The minute-taker needs to be seated in a position where she or he can see all the participants in the meeting.

At the beginning of the meeting it is important that a note is made of who:

- is present (hence the need for a signing in sheet to be completed – this will save time for the minute-taker in that it will already be written down)

- has sent apologies (the chairperson should state this at the beginning of the meeting)

- has failed to turn up (i.e. a person who was expected and has not sent apologies).

The minute-taker needs to allocate either one or two initials to each participant so that initial(s) can be put in a column when that person speaks rather than writing the full name. Again this is why it is useful to know in advance who might be present, so that some thought can be given to this in advance (especially if you have two participants with the same initials).

Taking notes

In an ideal world verbatim notes should be taken in a safeguarding adults meeting. However, the administrative person is only human and cannot be expected to write down every word. Shorthand was used by a lot of secretaries some time ago; some people who have the skills still use it and

✓

Subject:

Date: Time:

Name (please print)	Job title and organisation (if applicable)	Address, telephone number and email address

Figure 9.1 Example of a strategy meeting/case conference signing in sheet[1]

---

1   Signing in sheet will include sufficient lines for all delegates.

Type of meeting:

Date:

Duration:

Figure 9.2 Seating plan

that is fine. Nowadays there are many ways of learning how to speedwrite and various courses are widely available; however they cost fees which many organisations are not prepared to pay. Therefore, it is helpful if during training a potential minute-taker can be advised how to develop their own speedwriting techniques, which may involve developing their own ways of reducing words which are going to be heard many times in a meeting. It is important that a minute-taker develops their own way of remembering their shorthand and not be told what would be a good way of shortening a word; it has to be memorable and useful to the individual minute-taker.

It was said at the beginning of this chapter that the type of minutes taken for a safeguarding meeting are different to the minutes for a business meeting, which are very much action point orientated. The objective for a minute-taker in a safeguarding adults meeting is to try to record as much as possible (not all of which will appear in the final version of the shorter minutes) but an objective must be to ensure that the agreed actions have been recorded, that is, who is going to do what and within what timescale.

A minute-taker should always record the exact time the meeting started and finished. The actual time things happened during the meeting should also be recorded (e.g. when there was a break; when someone walked out, etc.).

A question which is asked frequently is, 'Why can't we use a tape recorder?' The main reasons why tape recorders are not used nowadays are two-fold. First, the person who transcribes the tape needs to be a trained audio typist. Transcribing is very time-consuming, even if one has the skills to do it. Second, it would be important for each participant to sign a consent form to say they agree to being taped during the meeting, but the form would also need to state very clearly how the tape would be used, accessed/transcribed by whom, where it would be stored and for how long.

Things said off the record

A good chairperson will have stated at the beginning of the meeting that nothing can be said off the record in such a meeting; everything which is said in a safeguarding adults meeting will be recorded. Where such a ground rule has not been set it can be difficult for the minute-taker to know what to record. This is the sort of issue which needs to be discussed between a chairperson and minute-taker before a meeting takes place. It has been known for some chairpersons to tell the minute-taker to take out certain things which were said because, 'That should never have been said'; 'we don't want him shown up in a bad light'; 'I don't want that person upset; we have to work with him in the future.' These excuses are not valid. If something is said it has to be recorded; the minutes have to be a true accurate record. Neither the chairperson nor the minute-taker can rewrite history. A police officer who attends strategy meetings and case conferences regularly experiences these problems:

Expert's experience and comment

Case conferences are always minuted, but my main issue is things are said and then I get the 4th or 5th version of it. People ask for things to be taken out. I have witnessed individuals make ridiculous statements at case conferences, which I have felt the need to challenge and subsequently the person asked for the original statement to be withdrawn from the minutes, which it was! I have experienced a lot of, 'This is not for the record,' which results in the minute-taker putting down their pencil.

Police Officer

Things shared under Section 115 of the Crime and Disorder Act 1998

Sometimes a chairperson will ask certain participants to go outside of the meeting room whilst certain information is shared. For example, the police may be sharing some information about a person's past offences which they might not want heard by the victim or certain other people. In other situations people will only share information with participants covered by Section 115 of the Crime and Disorder Act 1998, that is, where it is thought a crime has been committed or could be committed in the future a person can share information with personnel from the:

1. local authority

2. health authority

3. police

4. probation service.

So, in a safeguarding adults meeting any participants who are employed by an organisation in the voluntary or independent sectors would be asked to leave the meeting whilst that information was shared; afterwards they would then be allowed back into the meeting. The minute-taker should record:

- who went out of the meeting
- the times a person went out and came back (e.g. 'Mrs Marshall was asked to leave the room at 10.54; she came back in after the information had been shared at 11.12').

It is vital that a minute-taker knows that those participants who were absent for part of the meeting do *not* receive those parts of the minutes where the information was shared.

BEST PRACTICE POINTS

- State the exact time the meeting started and finished.
- Record what is said and by whom.
- Record any disagreements.
- Be exact about the balance of probabilities decisions (this will include names/numbers/percentages).
- Grading of risk of significant harm.
- Make sure you record in full all agreed actions, decisions and recommendations.
- Record the details of the safeguarding plan.
- Do not record repetitive statements – just note how many times it was repeated.
- Do not record what is already in written reports – but make sure you cross reference.

After the meeting

A chairperson should always formally debrief the minute-taker after the meeting has finished. There are many different reasons for this, many of which are not related to the subject of recording. However, what is important is that immediately after the meeting the chairperson should talk to the minute-taker about any problems they have had regarding the taking of minutes and the chairperson should also have a look at the notes which have been taken. This is the time that a minute-taker can raise any queries or concerns they may have. This is all part of maintaining a good working partnership between the chairperson and minute-taker, which will in turn help the process of producing good accurate minutes.

Writing up

A person who is required to produce minutes and who is reading this chapter will benefit from reading earlier chapters in the book. This is because some of the best practice points listed will be applicable when giving thought to producing minutes. The key things a minute-taker should think about are:

- preparation
- planning
- content
- layout
- drafting and redrafting.

As was noted at the beginning of the chapter, the standard of minutes can vary; this is often due to a lack of knowledge about how to take minutes during a meeting and what should be included in the final version of minutes for circulation. Geraldine Monaghan's experience is not unique to her local area:

Expert's experience and comment

Minute-taking – this needs sorting out. There is inconsistency in practice. Some minutes are a verbatim record as best they can be; others a simple statement of actions. It depends on the Chair. There is a need for clarity regarding the role of the Chair.

Geraldine Monaghan

Drafting minutes

Some safeguarding policies have templates for minutes which are to be circulated from strategy meetings and case conferences. There are pros and cons to developing templates. The advantages are that there is consistency in how minutes are produced and they help the minute-taker to focus on key subject areas. The disadvantages are that a template can be quite prescriptive and may not allow for the uniqueness of individual meetings or conferences. What follows is a checklist of what should be included in minutes, which should help a minute-taker draft the minutes which should eventually be shown to the chairperson.

BEST PRACTICE POINTS

- type of meeting – clear title linked to policy
- details of subject (name, date of birth, address)
- date
- duration
- venue
- people present – name, job title, organisation (or relationship to victim e.g. relative, neighbour)
- apologies
- absentees (i.e. people who failed to turn up on the day and did not send apologies)
- confidentiality statement
- dates of previous meetings (if applicable)
- previous minutes and matters arising (if applicable)
- presentation of reports
- key points from the discussions which took place
- agreements
- disagreements
- action points: name person responsible for carrying out each action and timescale
- balance of probabilities, that is, categories of abuse substantiated, not substantiated, inconclusive
- grading of risk/significant harm
- decisions and recommendations
- safeguarding plan
- date for review/next meeting.

It is really important for a minute-taker to be able to write up draft minutes in an environment which allows him or her to concentrate and focus; this is not always easy in many offices. In an ideal world the minute-taker should be allowed to set aside time specifically for the task of writing up in a place where there is a possibility of having some peace and quiet, with no interruptions or distractions. It is necessary to:

- Read through the notes taken in the meeting.

- Make a plan – consider the key points which need to be recorded.

- Decide on content.

- Decide on layout.

- Decide on appendices, that is, what will need to be attached to the minutes (e.g. reports, risk assessment, safeguarding plan).

- Ask for help if necessary, that is, talk to chairperson.

- Show the first draft to chairperson.

Layout

It has already been said that in some areas minute-takers will be required to work to a template for minutes. If there is no such pro-forma to work to, then the minute-taker has to think about layout in addition to content:

- make your own decision regarding layout

- some things are obligatory, for example, size of font

- headings and sub-headings

- numbering

- typing rules

- appendices.

Confidentiality and storage issues

Some local areas will have a confidentiality statement written in the Safeguarding Adults Policy and Procedures which is read out at the beginning of any safeguarding adults meeting. In this circumstance the confidentiality statement should be written at the top of the minutes. An example is given on p.191.

SOME BASIC TYPING RULES

1. HEADING 14 POINT BOLD

Text 12 point

Action 12 point italic

Sub-heading 12 point bold

Text 12 point

Action 12 point italic

2. HEADING (3 level)

Sub-heading

    (a) sub-subheading

3. HEADING (4 level)

Sub-heading

    3.1.1. sub-sub heading

        (a) sub-subheading

4. SPACES AND LINES

One space between words

Two spaces after a full stop, exclamation mark or question mark

One blank line between paragraphs and after a heading

Two blank lines between sections

Example confidentiality statement

This case conference is held under Churchtown's Safeguarding Adults Policy. The matters raised are confidential to the participants of the meeting/conference and the agencies they represent and will only be shared in the best interests of the vulnerable adult, and with their consent where it is appropriate to obtain it.

Minutes of the meeting are distributed on the understanding that they will be kept confidential and in a secure place.

In certain circumstances it may be necessary to make minutes of this meeting/conference available to solicitors, the civil and/or criminal courts, the Secretary of State in relation to the Protection of Vulnerable Adults Scheme, psychiatrists, professional staff employed by other social service agencies or other professionals involved in the welfare of the vulnerable adult(s). All such disclosures must be recorded.

The minutes of any safeguarding adults meeting should be stored in a safe place. In many organisations a worker will store them electronically, but as noted earlier in the book some organisations will keep paper records. Therefore, the minutes should only be accessible to those members of staff who need to see them.

Circulation

Once the final version of the minutes has been agreed, it is necessary to disseminate them as soon as possible using a safe method. Many statutory agencies disseminate information and documents by e-mail and can forget that not everyone has access to the Internet or has the use of e-mail in their workplace. It is important to remember that some organisations in the voluntary and independent sectors may not be using advanced technology; it is essential not to make assumptions. Therefore, the minute-taker must think about the different methods that can be used to disseminate minutes:

- Royal Mail postal services

- internal post systems

- e-mail, possibly with the minutes document being protected by a password to be circulated separately.

It is vital that whatever method is used, the word CONFIDENTIAL is used to maintain privacy.

Amendments

The chairperson should have explained in any meeting that if there are any errors or omissions in the minutes, then the chairperson should be made aware of these within a specified time limit (usually five working days after receipt). Sometimes participants contact the minute-taker to highlight any mistakes. The minute-taker should inform the chairperson of the comments or requests for amendments, but she or he cannot make any changes until the chairperson has agreed. If amendments are to be made the minutes will be retyped and then circulated again. The minutes should only be a record of what happened in the meeting. Things should not be taken out because a participant wished they had not said something. It has been known for participants to request information to be put in regarding events or incidents which have taken place after the meeting.

BEST PRACTICE POINTS

- Write up the minutes as soon as possible after the meeting.
- Record the minutes in the order of the agenda.
- Keep the layout simple.
- Be consistent in your use of headings, sub-headings, numbers, bullet points.
- Use full sentences, but do not make sentence too long.
- Write in the third person and use the past tense.
- Use plain language.
- Do not use jargon/abbreviations.
- Record the facts, namely, what was said and agreed.
- Do not be repetitious.
- Check you are not overusing certain words or phrases.
- Draft, check, redraft until you are happy with what you have produced.
- Discuss with the chairperson and don't be afraid to ask for help.
- Get the chairperson to sign off the final draft.
- Proofread the final version.
- Circulate within 10 working days.
- Use safe methods for circulation and mark **'CONFIDENTIAL'**.

Getting some practice

The old saying 'practice makes perfect' does have some relevance when developing minute-taking skills. If someone has been sent on a proper speedwriting course then they should have developed the necessary skills, but as was said earlier this does not happen very often in health and adult social care settings. Therefore, it is necessary to watch a simulation of a strategy meeting or case conference and try to minute-take.

EXERCISE 9.1

TAKING MINUTES

OBJECTIVE
To enable a worker to practise minute-taking.

PARTICIPANTS
Any number of workers can participate.

EQUIPMENT
Minute-taking book; pens; DVD with simulations of a case conference.[2]

TIME
5-minute simulation.

TASK
The worker takes minutes as they are watching/listening to the DVD.

NOTE FOR TRAINER
Many workers get disheartened or feel incompetent when they first participate in this exercise. It is necessary for them to undertake it several times during the course of a training day and to keep the simulations short. Participants usually develop their confidence during the course of the day.

---

2   For example: 'Case Conferences' – WAA4 DVD in the *Working with Adult Abuse Series* produced by Jacki Pritchard Ltd – see www.jackipritchard.co.uk.

EXERCISE 9.2

GETTING MORE PRACTICE

OBJECTIVE
To enable a worker to practise minute-taking in a more informal setting away from the workplace.

PARTICIPANTS
Individual.

EQUIPMENT
Minute-taking book; pens.

TIME
10 minutes every day.

TASK
A worker should set aside a 10-minute slot every day when they are either going to watch part of a television programme or listen to discussion (not music!!) on the radio. The idea is to take minutes of what is said in either situation. It is good to alternate between the two media, because when watching the television the worker will be observing as well as listening, which is what they should be doing in any safeguarding adults meeting.

EXERCISE 9.3

BAD EXAMPLES FOR CORRECTION

OBJECTIVE

To give examples of minutes which have been produced in different formats but which include some mistakes, bad practices, poor grammar and punctuation, etc. The worker is asked to produce a new set of minutes.

PARTICIPANTS

Individual.

EQUIPMENT

Paper and pens; bright highlighters. Three examples are given in Handouts 9.1; 9.2 and 9.3. These three handouts illustrate the different ways minutes can be presented, but all of them include mistakes, bad practices, etc.

TIME

30 minutes.

TASK

A worker is given one of the handouts to work on. They are asked to:

1. Highlight what they think are errors, the badly written parts, etc.

2. Rewrite the parts which need to be corrected or they think could be improved upon.

Handout 9.1

Bad example (1) for correction

Below you are given a list of the participants in an initial case conference followed by an extract taken from the early part of the conference.

MINUTES OF CASE CONFERENCE
SUBJECT: LAURA BENNETT (DOB: 25.6.30)
Address: 6 Norton Gardens, Churchtown

Date:	12th January 2009	
Duration:	11.00 to 13.05	
Venue:	Lounge 3, Summers Day EMI Home	
Present:		
Pat Edwards **(Chairperson)**	Team Manager, Older Persons Team, Churchtown SSD	PE
Sue Grant **(Minute-taker)**	Administrative Assistant, Churchtown SSD	SG
Amy Harrod **(Inquiry Officer)**	Social Worker, Older Persons Team, Churchtown SSD	AH
Sam Brown **(Inquiry Officer)**	Social Worker, Older Persons Team, Churchtown SSD	SB
Helen Goddard	Manager, Summer Days EMI Home, Amica Ltd	HG
Liz Smith	Manager, Fairfields Day Centre, Alzheimer's Society	LS
Errol King	Manager, Help For You Domiciliary Care Agency	EK
Angela Warren	Advocate, Churchtown Advocacy Service	AW
Apologies:		
David Michaels	Public Protection Unit, Churchtown Police	DM
Absent:		
Dr Paul Green	GP, Hanover Drive Surgery	PG

Ref	Item	Action

1. Introductions

Everyone introduced themselves. PE explained this was the initial case conference to be convened under Churchtown's Safeguarding Adults Multi-Agency Policy and Procedures regarding allegations that Mrs Laura Bennett had been physically assaulted. She read out the usual definitions and ground rules and reminded people that they should have put two hours aside for the meeting. EK became stroppy even before the meeting started saying didn't people realise he is very busy and had rotas to organise before 4.00 and has not got the time to sit in meetings which are a waste of time anyway. PE looked EK in the eye and reminded him that when there is an allegation of abuse an investigation has to be undertaken and a case conference is part of that process EK looked away and said nothing else.

2. Minutes of Strategy Meeting on 16 December 2008

PE asked me to distribute the minutes of the meeting because some people had said when invited to the case conference they had never received copies. As Christmas has just been and gone it may be due to the post and things getting lost. Everyone read the minutes. AW said she had received her copy and had shared it with Mrs Bennett as she was surprised no-one had discussed the meeting with her. EK laughed and said what was the point in doing that as Mrs Bennett 'is nutty as a fruit cake'. AW said she found that comment offensive. EK shrugged his shoulders, looked at me and said 'You better not record it then'. PE came in here and said everything in a case conference has to be minuted. We then moved on to the next item.

3. Inquiry Officers Report

AH said she was going to talk to the report (Appendix 2) which had been prepared by herself and the other Inquiry Officer SB. She reminded everyone that the alert had come through to the EDT on Sunday night 14 December. At that time Mrs Bennett was having respite care in Summer Days EMI Home, whilst her son and daughter in law were in Benidorm – taking a well earned break before Christmas. No-one went out from EDT and information was passed on to the OPT on the Monday morning. The original alert was that Mrs Bennett had sustained injuries during the night and it was suspected that another resident, Oscar Riding, had gone into Mrs Bennett's room which he frequently does. HG chipped in and said from what her night staff told her she was 'disgusted' with the attitude of the EDT worker who seemed to think that there was no sense of urgency because Mrs Bennett would not remember anything because of her Alzheimer's. EK came in again and said 'Well that's right isn't it?' PE corrected EK again.

✓

Bad example (2) for correction

Below you are given a list of the participants in a review case conference followed by an extract taken from later in the conference.

Greenflats Safeguarding Adults Policy

Case Conference 3

Re: Barry Jordan (known as Baza)

Date of Birth: 23.9.89

Accommodated at: 39 Marsh Lane, Fenland, Greenflats GR18 9DF (Harico Ltd)

Date of this conference: 12th January 2009, held at Marsh Lane

Time started: 9.30

Those Present:

Service user	Barry Jordan
Independent Chairperson	Milburn Porter, Team Manager, LD, Greenflats Adult Social Care
Keyworker	Alison Yates, Social Worker, LD, Adult Social Care
Primary Worker	Julia Merrick, Support Worker, Harico Ltd
Police	Mick Denver, CID, Greenflats Police HQ
Psychologist	Marvin Keyes, Psychology Unit, Greenflats NHS Trust
Advocate	Lauren Payne, Greenflats Advocacy Service

Apologies from:

Nurse	Selina Grey, LD, Greenflats Adult Social Care (on long term sick leave)

<u>Summary from Chairperson</u>

Milburn thanked everyone for their contributions and said that it had been helpful to have detailed reports in order to make the decision whether this case could be closed under Safeguarding.

He said the main points made were:

- It has been confirmed by Mick that the CPS are going to proceed with the case and Joan Anderson has been charged with theft.

- Joan has been referred to the temporary POVA List.

- Alison and Selina between them have continued to visit on a weekly basis (until Selina went off sick) and were pleased with Baza's progress. His fear of going out has reduced and he has gone back to some of his usual activities.

- Julia is also positive regarding Barry's progress but feels he needs more one to one as he still has panic attacks regularly.

- Marvin feels a lot more work needs to be done in the future regarding Baza's fear and panic attacks.

- Lauren has supported Barry through the investigation and feels that she no longer has a role to play as Barry is well supported by others.

- Barry said that he is still scared of Joan and does not like to go out alone.

Decision

Milburn asked the participants if they were in agreement that this case should be closed under SOVA. Barry became upset at this point because he misunderstood the proposal. Break taken: 10.10 to 10.15. Milburn repeated the proposal and it was a unanimous decision that Barry's case would closed under SOVA but would remain open to the LD team.

Recommendations

1. No further action needed under Safeguarding.

2. Alison will continue to visit Barry on a monthly basis.

3. A new nurse from the LD needs to be allocated.

4. Marvin will continue to see Baza on a weekly basis.

5. Advocacy support will be withdrawn.

6. Police will keep ASC and Havico infirmed re the progression of the case to court.

Time conference finished: 10.25

Minute-taker: Simon Jeffies, Admin, Greenflats Safeguarding Unit

Handout 9.3

Bad example (3) for correction

Below you are given an extract from the later part of a case conference.

Item 10: Substantiation of allegations of abuse

Chair asked for each category to be considered: substantiated, not substantiated, inconclusive.

Physical – substantiated (everyone agreed except 1)

Emotional – long discussion, disagreements – went 51% maj. Not substantiated

Discriminatory – ditto!!

Item 11: Risk of significant harm for future

Victim wants to remain in situ.

High risk case.

Need to monitor for more injuries.

DC to keep an eye open. Use bodymaps as and when.

Item 12: Safeguarding Plan

As above

Item 13: Review

When SW thinks necessary.

AOB

No

Suggested reading

For general note-taking and minute-taking (*not* for safeguarding adults work):

Gutmann, J. (2006) *Taking Minutes of Meetings.* 2nd edition. London: Kogan Page.

Kesselman-Turkel, J. and Peterson, F. (2003) *Note-Taking Made Easy.* Wisconsin: University of Wisconsin.

We suggest that a worker should read their local Safeguarding Adults Policy and Procedure to check whether there is any specific guidance about the minutes which should be produced from any strategy meeting or case conference.

Chapter 10

Report Writing for Court

In earlier chapters in this book we have seen that good quality recording is crucial to the process of safeguarding adults. Evidence of abuse and neglect needs to be carefully catalogued, together with a range of contextual information about the person themselves, their carers and family and the forms of support which have been offered. As we have seen, this information is recorded for a number of purposes and audiences. Arguably the most important of these, and certainly the most challenging is a court hearing for purposes of deciding about the care or welfare of a vulnerable adult. This chapter concerns the process of using case recording to produce a statement or report which will help the court in its difficult decision-making.

Before sitting down to write a statement or report for court, it is important to think about a few preliminary points. Some of these are legal rules about what amounts to evidence that the court can take account of – rules about what is admissible. No less important are the practical questions of how to organise and present the material as a coherent, persuasive document for court, together with who will use the report, and in what way.

Admissibility – what evidence can the court accept?

As we saw in Chapter 5, the standard of proof depends on the type of proceedings. In criminal proceedings (proceedings brought for a criminal offence), the prosecution have to prove the charge 'beyond reasonable doubt'. In civil proceedings, the court has to find things proved on a balance of probabilities. Civil proceedings include, for example, an application in the High Court to decide the best interests of someone who lacks capacity to decide for themselves.

Hearsay

A court report needs to be clear whether events related are the person's own direct evidence, or have been witnessed by someone else. In *criminal* proceedings there is a strict rule that a witness (A) can generally only give evidence about things they have heard and seen themselves. Reporting what someone else has told them is hearsay and is inadmissible. A cannot tell a criminal court what B has heard or seen, only B can do that.

Hearsay is defined as 'That which one hears or has heard someone say' (Oxford English Dictionary). Hearsay evidence is 'The evidence of those who relate, not what they know themselves, but what they have heard from others' (The Free Dictionary undated).

In *civil* proceedings the court can admit hearsay evidence, but it will carry less weight. So if someone makes a disclosure to the report writer, it will be more compelling if they make a statement to the court themselves rather than through the report writer. There may be very good reasons why an alleged victim cannot make their own statement – they may lack the capacity to do this, or despite the available reassurance and support they may be unable to face the court situation. If they cannot make a statement, or it would be against their best interests to be put through the ordeal of court, the report should explain this.

A report quoting hearsay information should say who provided it, their name and, if a professional, the post they hold and their agency. Occasionally, a source should be kept anonymous, but this should be explained, and exceptional. Saying where information was obtained enables the court and parties to trace back to its source. Citing one's sources is a requirement, as well as making the reported information more believable. It also helps flag up those cases where the writer is not necessarily vouching for the information, but passing on what they have been told.

Example of good report writing

A report might say of a carer, 'Mrs Smith feels she does not receive enough support from other family members or from social care.' If this is changed to 'Mrs Smith *tells me* she feels she does not receive enough support...' – this makes clear where the information has come from, and subtly puts important distance between the writer and Mrs Smith's feelings about her caring role.

Indirect evidence is often sufficient for a first hearing, particularly one which takes place in an emergency. By the time of the final hearing, the court will expect the most direct evidence we can obtain.

Relevance

Evidence is only admissible if it is relevant to the issues before the court. In cases concerning the welfare of vulnerable adults, a wide range of information is likely to be relevant to the court's enquiries about their needs and the best way of meeting these. However, there is a relatively small category of information which may not be relevant. Report writers should be particularly careful about including or over-emphasising material which may reflect badly on someone but not help much with deciding the crucial issues in the case.

Fact and opinion

The language used in the report should make clear what is 'fact' and what is opinion. A fact is the direct observation of the senses, what has been heard or seen. Opinion is an interpretation of those facts. Opinion can only be offered by a witness who is qualified by training or experience to give that particular opinion. Remember also that opinions are personal to the witness. They should be expressed as the writer's view rather than those of the agency or department.

For example, a lay person who observes a bruise can describe it by size and colour and the use of a bodymap. However, only a suitably qualified clinician is able to offer the court an opinion about the likely age of the bruise, the force needed to cause it, or the plausibility of any account of how it may have been caused.

Example of good report writing

Language can be used to help flag up for the reader the difference between hearsay and the writer's own observations; and between fact and opinion.

For example: 'On 13 August 2011, I received a telephone call from Ms D, manager at the Acorns Day Centre, that Ms X had arrived with them that morning with four small bruises to her left cheekbone.' This is factual evidence. It does not offer interpretation. However it is not the writer's own direct information, it is hearsay. The wording makes clear how, when and from whom it was obtained.

An opinion which the writer has the training or experience to give can be introduced by saying, 'It is my view that ...', 'In my opinion...'

Seeing the report in context

It is also worth thinking about how a report provided for the court will be used, and how it fits in with all the other evidence available to the court.

A written statement or report is only part of a witness's evidence for court. This is because everyone who provides evidence in writing must make themselves available to be called to give oral evidence at the hearing if required. If any other party wishes to challenge a fact or opinion in the report, they may require the report writer to attend court to answer questions. If on the other hand all parties accept the report, there will be no need for its report writer to give oral evidence.

Where facts or opinions are not agreed, it will be for the court to hear from all parties and witnesses, and decide which evidence to prefer. At the end of the hearing, the court will make findings, explaining which facts and opinions it adopts in coming to a decision. This brings us back to the point that the more solidly documented and explained the report is, the more likely it is to be accepted by the court, and to help the court in the difficult decision(s) that have to be made.

Even the report writer of the most authoritative report is liable to be asked questions at the court hearing. However, it will also be apparent that a poorly argued or documented report is generally even more likely to lead to challenging, if not hostile cross-examination. Hence in writing reports for court, it is important to ask oneself, 'How will I defend or back up this point if asked about it at court?'

Back to purpose

The purpose of a statement or report for court may sound obvious. One may have been instructed by one's agency to write it, or directed by the court. But although that may be the reason for the report, it is not its purpose. Being clear about purpose:

BEST PRACTICE POINTS

Purpose:
- helps the reader by flagging up what to look for in the report; and
- helps the writer by focusing attention on what is relevant and the order and structure in which to set it out.

So at an early point the report should state its purpose. This might be, for example:
- to update the court on events since the writer's last statement and to provide an assessment and proposed care plan; OR
- to place before the court one's account of a spontaneous disclosure.

It is necessary to revisit some important questions:

KEY QUESTIONS
- Who is going to read this report?
- What format is required?
- What style of writing should be adopted?

Because we are concerned with adult abuse and safeguarding adults it is imperative that the writer remains focused on the six main categories of abuse as well as other important definitions of abuse which are defined in *No Secrets* as:

DEFINITIONS OF ABUSE

- *physical*
- *sexual*
- *financial/material*
- *emotional*
- *neglect/act of omission*
- *discriminatory*
- *institutional abuse*
- *stranger abuse.*

(DH 2000)

Unfortunately, some statements and reports for court suggest that the writer did not have a clear focus or plan before sitting down to write. Unless all the content addresses the report's purpose in a clear, logical way the reader may find it hard to follow and the report will fail in its over-riding objective, which is to inform and persuade.

Report writing considerations

There are a number of practical issues worth considering before putting pen to paper. Taking time to address these issues should not only produce a better report, but actually save time in the long run.

Planning and forethought

Time taken thinking about what to say in a report, and how to present it, is time well spent. There is a temptation to begin writing before the content and structure have been thought through.

It is a good idea to start – if possible, well ahead of time – by noting down ideas about incidents and concerns that need to be included, and then thinking about the best order in which to arrange them. Sometimes a report will have a separate chronology of involvement and significant events appended. If not, there should be a chronological section in the report which provides the reader with a clear account of the key events in the case and their sequence. This should be closely based on the file chronology discussed in Chapter 5.

In addition to the chronology, the report should address the evidence by topic. The topic headings will be dictated by the individual case, but might include for example physical neglect, sexual abuse, or support previously offered and its impact.

In noting down points to include in the report, it is helpful to think about which section each point belongs in.

BEST PRACTICE POINTS

- Plan plenty of time to write a report.
- Think about where to write, whether in the office or elsewhere.
- Blank sufficient time free of other diary commitments.
- It is helpful to allow time to re-draft, and for one's supervisor and legal adviser to read through.
- Allow time to amend in light of their comments.
- As a rule of thumb, a first draft report should be ready at least 7 to 10 days before the filing date set by the court.

Structure and content

The opening of a report for court should introduce the writer (including their professional qualifications and experience), and the person or family being written about. As we saw above, it should state the purpose of the report. At the end the conclusions and recommendations should be set out, with explanation – what is being recommended and why.

Order

It is important to think about the most logical, accessible order in which to present information in the report. Usually, the narrative information is presented first, followed by sections covering assessment, conclusions and recommendations.

Dates and times, locations and people

When referring to an incident, make clear when (and where) it took place, and who was present.

Layout

The report should be divided up into numbered sections, each with a heading that guides the reader's attention from one topic to the next in a logical way.

A clear, logical structure is crucial to enable the report writer to get their thoughts and information in order; and so that the reader can follow the thread, and refer back as necessary. For the same reason, the pages should be numbered, as should the sections and paragraphs. This has the added advantages of ease of reference later, including at the court hearing, and of making the report look organised and authoritative. For example, consider this opening to one section of a report:

Example of report writing

3 Neglect suffered
In this section I summarise the evidence of neglect Mrs X has suffered while at home.

3.1 Physical neglect
[this sub-section might refer to the ways in which Mrs X's physical needs have not been met]

3.2 Emotional neglect
[this sub-section could include ways in which Mrs X's emotional needs, for example for stimulation and companionship, have not been met]

Heading and numbering the sections and sub-sections in this way makes the material easier to follow and refer back to. Particularly with abuse and neglect, this topical arrangement helps make clear any pattern or repetition in the way the person has been treated.

BEST PRACTICE POINTS

- Start thinking well in advance about the content and structure of a report for court.
- Jot down ideas for inclusion as they occur.
- Consider using Mind Maps to help decide 'what goes where' in the overall structure of the report, and to ensure that the reader is able to follow the thread.
- Consider what supporting information may be needed to back up points made, particularly if they are likely to be contentious.
- If time allows, don't be afraid to re-phrase or re-jig content if on reading through you find a better way to express it.

Relevant detail

A full, balanced picture should be presented to the court. In relation to each incident and concern, it is helpful to think about the level of detail the reader will need to appreciate its significance and place it in context.

Example of report writing

Consider this excerpt from an account in a report of a pre-arranged visit to Ms B, who provides domiciliary care to Mrs A, whose daughter has complained about sums of money apparently going missing. Think what might be added in order to provide full detail and context.

> I explained to Ms B that some money seemed to have gone astray at Ms A's home. Ms B replied that she never handles money for

Mrs A, and understands her daughter does this; and that she has only once seen money in the house – a £20 note left on the kitchen counter some 4 weeks ago, which she had given to Mrs A.

This account is good, in that it lets the carer 'speak for herself', apparently containing a full account of what Ms B said in her defence. On the other hand the opening sentence is lacking in detail and context, because it does not record if Ms B was told how much money had gone missing or on what occasion(s).

BEST PRACTICE POINTS

In devising a structure for a court report, it is important to include:

- court heading – a standard format, setting out the name of the court and case number, the parties and the title of the report or statement
- introduction – the author's name, qualifications and length of experience, current position and role in the case; the purpose of the statement or report
- family composition/genogram
- 'pen picture' of service user – their strengths, needs, vulnerabilities and support network
- chronology of involvement/significant events (unless a separate chronology is being filed)
- physical abuse – evidence for it, and assessment of its severity and impact on the service user
- neglect – evidence and severity
- sexual abuse
- financial abuse
- support provided and its impact
- what the court is being asked to do – why it is the least restrictive alternative
- care and support plan
- signature and date.

Style of writing

Reports should be written in a formal style, even if the content is personal and sensitive. But formal does not have to mean complicated. Straightforward, direct language is usually more persuasive and accessible. Consider the following extract from a conclusion to a report for court:

Example of bad and good report writing

> I have taken cognisance of the possibilities that a package involving enhanced support might succeed in procuring the sufficient alleviation of risk to Ms X for which we have been striving; and, on the other hand that the point has now been reached such that the only adequate guarantee of her safety would be an order authorising her removal from her current environment, and am inclined to favour the latter, quite strongly.

What would have been better:

This could be the writer's natural style. It could be how they think court reports should be worded. However, the sentence is far too long, and the language much too complicated to be easily understood. It has to be read several times to be comprehended. It is even more important in safeguarding than other contexts that we use direct, clear, precise language. Without losing too much detail, this sentence could be re-written:

> I have considered carefully whether Ms X could be kept safe by providing enhanced support. On balance it is my view that she will only be safe if removed from her current environment.

This second version uses fewer than half the number of words. It is also much clearer, and therefore safer because it can be more easily understood and acted upon.

Evidence suggesting abuse

Any information which suggests the person has been abused or neglected should be included. It is important to explain the basis of any professional opinion that a particular change in behaviour may suggest abuse. The account should also consider other possible explanations, and say which explanation is the most likely, and why. Consider this case example:

Example of good report writing

The chronology makes clear that when Mr D attended the day centre between 1 April and 15 May, he was more withdrawn and less communicative than usual. This change in demeanour could have been for a number of reasons. These would include that he was worried about something or that the centre's regime had changed. However, when I consider his later disclosures and his physical injuries and their timing, it seems to me most likely that he was subdued at this time because of the abuse he was experiencing. I base this view on my knowledge of Mr D and my experience working with other adults with learning disabilities in the past.

In this example, the report writer has considered alternative explanations for the change observed in Mr D's behaviour and has explained why she thinks the change was because of abuse. If the writer is drawing a conclusion which is likely to be contentious, it is even more important to explain that conclusion carefully.

Wishes and feelings of the victim/other people

It is important that the report sets out the views of the service user about what has happened to them and what is proposed. The results of the assessment of the service user's mental capacity should be set out. The account of any alleged perpetrator should also be carefully considered. The views of carers and other family members are also crucial.

Example of report writing

After recording a disclosure by the service user (Mr M) against his wife and carer, the report writer might go on to say:

Mr M told me that the abuse had come as a shock and had made him feel frightened, isolated and humiliated. His daughter told me she had always seen her parents as having a close, mutually supportive relationship and she had had no reason to suspect her father was being abused. Mrs M described her husband as having become increasingly demanding to care for, but denied she had ever used abusive language or behaviour towards him.

Care plan or support plan

The care or support plan should follow logically from the assessment of needs and risks. It should have been explored in some detail, including approval of funding and the actual availability of the proposed placement and care package at the time they will be needed. Care or support plans presented to court may be similar to the safeguarding plans discussed in Chapter 8 previously. With plans presented to court, it is important they are robust and carefully thought through, and that they can withstand challenge from the other parties at court. If the proposal involves removing the person from their home, or not returning them there, this step should be very carefully explained and justified, particularly if either the service user or a family member has reservations or is opposed to the plan. The court will need to be satisfied that the person could not be kept safe at home and that removal is the 'least restrictive option'.

Conclusion

Many adult safeguarding situations can be resolved without needing to go to court. Indeed, there are many people for whom a more enduring solution to the risks they face can be achieved by working on a co-operative basis with their carers and family, and sometimes even with someone suspected of having abused them. But there is a small minority of people who can in the end only be protected by taking the matter to court.

Writing a report for court proceedings can appear a daunting task, particularly if one has not been involved in the court arena before. However, a report which succeeds in informing and persuading the court and parties is likely to be one which applies the good practice steps suggested throughout this book – recording and explaining carefully, clearly and logically and thinking about how one's message is likely to come across. A carefully written report can reflect well on the writer and their agency and profession, as well as contributing to effective safeguarding of an adult at risk.

Suggested reading

If at all possible we suggest that the reader should try to access some court reports which have been written (by staff in their own agency) and read them, bearing in mind the best practice which has been suggested in this chapter.

References

Action on Elder Abuse (2006) *Adult Protection Data Collection and Reporting Requirements.* London: AEA.

Association of Directors of Social Services (2005) *Safeguarding Adults: A National Framework of Standards for Good Practice and Outcomes in Adult Protection Work.* London: ADSS.

Commission for Social Care Inspection, Association of Directors of Social Services and Association of Chief Police Officers (2007) *Safeguarding Adults Protocols and Guidance.* London: CSCI.

Crime and Disorder Act (1998) London: HMSO.

Crown Prosecution Service (2004) *The Code for Crown Prosecutors.* London: CPS.

Davies, M. (1993) 'Recognizing Abuse: An Assessment Tool for Nurses.' In P. Decalmer and F. Glendenning (eds) *The Mistreatment of Elderly People.* London: Sage.

Davies, M. (1997) 'Key Issues for Nursing: The Need to Challenge Practice.' In P. Decalmer and F. Glendenning (eds) *The Mistreatment for Elderly People.* 2nd edition. London: Sage.

Department for Constitutional Affairs (2006) *A Guide to the Human Rights Act 1998.* 3rd Edition. London: DCA.

Department of Health (1991) *Care Management and Assessment: Practitioners' Guide.* London: Department of Health Social Services Inspectorate.

Department of Health (2000) *No Secrets: Guidance on Developing and Implementing Multi-agency Policies and Procedures to Protect Vulnerable Adults from Abuse.* London: DH.

Dictionary.com (undated) 'Confidentiality.' Available at http://dictionary.reference.com/browse/confidentiality, accessed on 27 September 2010.

Domestic Violence, Crime and Victims Act (2004) London: The Stationery Office.

Fulmer, T. (1984) 'Elder abuse assessment tool.' *Dimensions of Critical Care Nursing 3,* 4, 216–20.

Hartman, A. (1995) 'Diagrammatic assessment of family relationships.' *Families in Society 76,* 111–122.

HM Government (2010) *Working Together to Safeguard Children.* London: The Stationery Office.

Hilton, C. and Hyder, M. (1992) *Getting to Grips with Punctuation and Grammar.* London Letts.

Human Rights Act (1998) London: HMSO.

Laming, Lord (June 2003) *The Victoria Climbié Report.* London: The Stationery Office.

Laming, Lord (2009) *The Protection of Children in England: A Progress Report.* London: The Stationary Office.

Mackay, K. (2008) 'Scottish Legislative Framework for Supporting and Protecting Adults.' In J. Pritchard (ed.) *Good Practice in the Law and Safeguarding Adults.* London: Jessica Kingsley Publishers.

Mandelstam, M. (1998) *An A–Z of Community Care Law.* London: Jessica Kingsley Publishers.

McGoldrick, M. and Gerson, R. (1985) *Genograms in Family Assessment.* New York: W.W. Norton and Company.

National Assembly for Wales (2000) *In Safe Hands. Implementing Adult Protection Procedures in Wales.* Cardiff: National Assembly for Wales.

NHS and Community Care Act (1990) London: HMSO.

Pritchard, J. (1996) *Working with Elder Abuse: A Training Manual for Home Care, Residential and Day Care Staff.* London: Jessica Kingsley Publishers.

Pritchard, J. (2000) *The Needs of Older Women: Services for Victims of Elder Abuse and Other Abuse.* Bristol: The Policy Press.

Pritchard, J. (2001) *Becoming A Trainer in Adult Abuse Work.* London: Jessica Kingsley Publishers.

Pritchard, J. (2003) *Support Groups for Older People Who Have Been Abused: Beyond Existing.* London: Jessica Kingsley Publishers.

Pritchard, J. (2007) *Working with Adult Abuse: A Training Manual for People Working with Vulnerable Adults.* London: Jessica Kingsley Publishers.

Pritchard, J. (2008) *Good Practice in Safeguarding Adults: Working Effectively in Adult Protection.* London: Jessica Kingsley Publishers.

Pritchard, J. and Sainsbury, E. (2004) *Can You Read Me?: Creative Writing with Child and Adult Victims of Abuse.* London: Jessica Kingsley Publishers.

Reder, P and Duncan, S. (1999) *Lost Innocents: A Follow Up Study of Fatal Child Abuse.* London: Routledge.

Reder, P., Duncan, S. and Gray, M. (1993) *Beyond Blame: Child Abuse Tragedies Revisited.* London: Routledge.

Ross, M., Ross, P.A. and Ross, M.C. (1985) 'Abuse of the Elderly.' *The Canadian Nurse 81,* 2, 36– 39.

The Free Dictionary (undated) 'Hearsay evidence.' Available at http://legal-dictionary. thefreedictionary.com/hearsay+evidence, accessed on 27 September 2010.

Thomas, H. (2010) 'Mini Mental State Examination.' Patient UK website. Available at www.patient.co.uk/doctor/Mini-Mental-State-Examination-(MMSE).htm, accessed on 14 September 2010.

Index